HOTSPOTS
GRAN CANARIA

Thomas Cook

GW00640723

Written by Brian and Eileen Anderson, updated by Ann Smith
Front cover photography courtesy of Thomas Cook Tour Operations Ltd

Original concept by Studio 183 Limited
Series design by Bridgewater Books
Cover design/artwork by Lee Biggadike, Studio 183 Limited

Produced by the Bridgewater Book Company
The Old Candlemakers, West Street, Lewes, East Sussex BN7 2NZ, United Kingdom
www.bridgewaterbooks.co.uk
Project Editor: Emily Casey Bailey
Project Designer: Lisa McCormick

Published by Thomas Cook Publishing
A division of Thomas Cook Tour Operations Limited
PO Box 227, Units 15-16, Coningsby Road, Peterborough PE3 8SB, United Kingdom
email: books@thomascook.com
www.thomascookpublishing.com
+ 44 (0) 1733 416477

ISBN-13: 978-1-84157-524-7
ISBN-10: 1-84157-524-0

First edition © 2006 Thomas Cook Publishing
Text © 2006 Thomas Cook Publishing
Maps © 2006 Thomas Cook Publishing
Head of Thomas Cook Publishing: Chris Young
Project Editor: Diane Ashmore
Production/DTP Editor: Steven Collins

Printed and bound in Spain by Graficas Cems, Navarra, Spain

All rights reserved. No part of this publication may be reproduced, stored in a retrieval system or transmitted, in any form or by any means, electronic, mechanical, recording or otherwise, in any part of the world, without prior permission of the publisher. Requests for permission should be made to the publisher at the above address.

Although every care has been taken in compiling this publication, and the contents are believed to be correct at the time of printing, Thomas Cook Tour Operations Limited cannot accept any responsibility for errors or omission, however caused, or for changes in details given in the guidebook, or for the consequences of any reliance on the information provided. Descriptions and assessments are based on the author's views and experiences when writing and do not necessarily represent those of Thomas Cook Tour Operations Limited.

CONTENTS

SYMBOLS KEY

The following is a key to the symbols used throughout this book:

i	information office	🛍	shopping
🚌	bus stop	🍴	restaurant
✉	post office	▣	café
✝	church	🍸	bar
🛡	police station	◉	fine dining
↘	tip		

---

t telephone   **f** fax   **e** email   **w** website address

a address   **o** opening times   **❶** important

€ budget price   **€€** mid-range price   **€€€** most expensive

★ specialist interest   **★★** see if passing   **★★★** top attraction

---

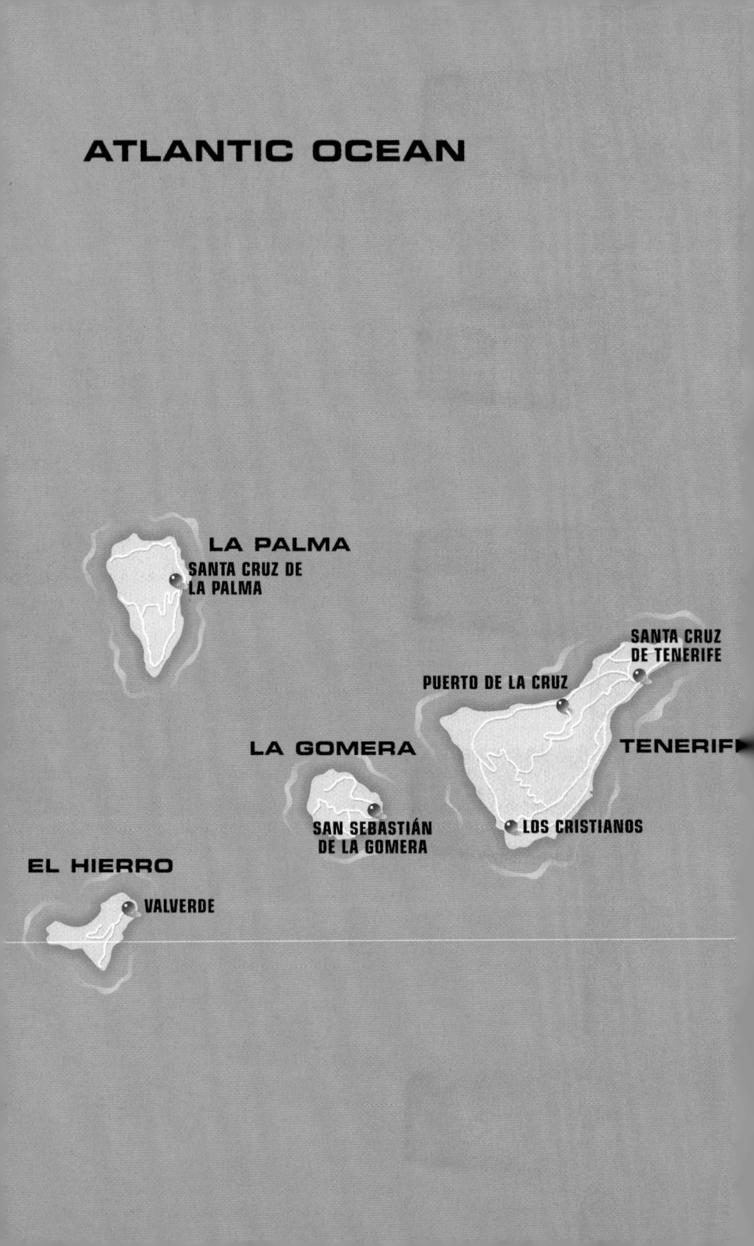

ATLANTIC OCEAN

LA PALMA

SANTA CRUZ DE
LA PALMA

SANTA CRUZ
DE TENERIFE

PUERTO DE LA CRUZ

LA GOMERA

TENERIF

SAN SEBASTIÁN
DE LA GOMERA

LOS CRISTIANOS

EL HIERRO

VALVERDE

NORTH
AMERICA

EUROPE

CANARY
ISLANDS

AFRICA

SOUTH
AMERICA

LANZAROTE

ARRECIFE

PLAYA BLANCA

PUERTO DEL
CARMEN

CORRALEJO

FUERTEVENTURA

PUERTO DEL
ROSARIO

GRAN TARAJAL

JANDÍA PLAYA

LAS PALMAS DE GRAN CANARIA

GRAN CANARIA

UERTO DE MOGÁN

N

| 0 | 25 | 50 km |
| 0 | | 30 miles |

Getting to know Gran Canaria

The Canaries are divided into Eastern and Western provinces, with Gran Canaria in the east (along with Lanzarote and Fuerteventura) and Tenerife in the west (with the smaller islands of La Gomera, El Hierro and La Palma). The islands of the eastern province have a hot, dry African climate, which makes them different in character from the wetter and greener islands of the western province. The massive dune systems at Maspalomas, on Gran Canaria, are a continuation of the Saharan desert, yet this island's high volcanic peaks can also be covered in snow in the winter.

Gran Canaria is the third largest of the Canary Islands (see map, page 10), at 1560 sq km (969 sq miles), sharing the status of joint capital of the Canaries with neighbouring Tenerife. In terms of population, it is the largest, since 50 per cent (around 953,462 people, with an average age of 34.8) of the total population of the Canaries lives here. The island is frequently described as a miniature continent – not just because of the variety of its landscapes, but also because of the large African population, which lends additional colour to a vibrant Hispanic culture.

Gran Canaria's year-round warmth brings holidaymakers from all over Europe, intent on making the most of a one- or two-week break. And for those who want to build up a suntan, Gran Canaria allows you to to do it in style. Apart from great beaches of golden sand, with the sun never too far away, there are plenty of other exciting places to pitch a towel or find a sunbed – on the decks of a catamaran sailing the Atlantic, perhaps, or in the privacy of a huge sand dune where you can (literally) let it all hang out. Gran Canaria also attracts people who want to escape from the crowded beaches and enjoy a measure of solitude. The island is excellent for walking, with spectacular volcanic landscapes to explore in the mountainous interior, as well as wild and undeveloped beaches (many with excellent fish restaurants) in the north.

THE SPORTING LIFE

Gran Canaria is perfect for water sports. The way that the island dips from north to south has created gently shelving beaches in the south, ideal for swimmers and novice windsurfers. In the north, Atlantic swells break against buried reefs to create waves mighty enough to attract keen surfers. If you want to try your hand at sailing, or the more relaxed pursuit of deep-sea fishing, all the opportunities are there. Sports enthusiasts are catered for, with chances to play golf, enjoy some fine walking, go horse riding or even ride a camel!

SHOPPERS' PARADISE

For those in search of retail therapy, this island is the nearest thing to heaven. It was made just for you! Shopping centres abound – with 14 in the resort of Playa del Inglés alone. The island is a vast, duty-free emporium with plenty of bargains to be had – although you will need to test your skills at haggling in the main tourist resorts.

LUNAR LANDSCAPES

On the drive from airport to resort, visitors often comment on the peculiar landscape, likening it to the moon. The hot, dry lower slopes are particularly barren and it is hard to believe that the interior hides spectacular landscapes – but it certainly does! Roughly circular in shape, the whole of the central region is mountainous. The highest peak reaches an altitude of almost 1919 m (6300 ft). Shaped and sculptured by the erosive forces of nature, the island boasts deep ravines, or *barrancos*, that rise high into the mountains and lead in breathtaking descent towards the sea.

THE PERFECT CLIMATE

Trade winds blowing from the north-east control the island's climate for most of the year. The mountains trap most of the moisture out of the winds as cloud, leaving the south to enjoy the very best of the island's sunshine. Sheltered areas in the south claim as many as 350 sunny days in every year.

Thanks again to the trade winds, the island's climate is gentle throughout all seasons, with summer temperatures around 23–25°C (73–77°F) and winter just two or three degrees cooler. As the variation in

ATLANTIC OCEAN

LAS PALMAS

GALDAR
Guia
Cenobio de Valerón
ARUCAS
TAMARACEITE
AGAETE
FIRGAS
Jardin Botánico Canario
GC3
TAFIRA BAJA
TEROR
VALLESECO
SANTA BRÍGIDA
TAFIRA ALTA
216 m
ARTENARA
LAS LAGUNETAS
SAN MATEO
LA ATALAYA
Cruz de Tejeda
SAN NICOLÁS DE TOLENTINO
Roque Bentayga
TEJEDA
Degollada de Beccerra
TELDE
Roque Nublo 813 m
Cuarto Puertos
AYACATA
1949 m
Barranco de Guayadeque
Museo di Piedras
Cruz Grande
INGENIO
SANTA LUCIA
AGÜIMES
CARRIZAL
SAN BARTOLOME DE TIRAJANA
Forteleza de Ansite
MOGÁN
FATAGA
Fataga Valley
Parque de Cocodrilo
586 m
Palmitos Park
ARTEARA
PUERTO DE MOGÁN
Mundo Aborigen
PUERTO RICO
Sioux City
SAN AGUSTIN
Pasito Blanco
ARGUINEGUIN
PLAYA DEL INGLÉS
MASPALOMAS

N

0   5   10 km
0   5 miles

ATLANTIC OCEAN

10

temperature is so small, some winter days can be warmer than some summer days. The near constant winds temper the heat. Puerto Rico, located south west, is often sheltered from breezes and is a good place to head for on days when the breeze is too strong.

FLORA

The flora on the island is unique and very different to that seen in the Mediterranean. Palm trees are very much at home and grow freely in all parts. They are used extensively for shade and decoration in and around resorts. The cactus-like *Euphorbia canariensis* is a common plant of dry hillsides and could easily be called the 'candlestick plant'. Garden plants are usually much more familiar, especially bougainvillea, seen in a variety of colours, as well as hibiscus and the colourful poinsettia, which grows to tree size on Gran Canaria.

The best of Gran Canaria

Gran Canaria offers a whole range of fascinating and fun things to see and do.

Visit Las Palmas There is almost too much to see, with the old historical centre, the upmarket shopping streets and the resort beach itself. Two different itineraries are suggested (pages 14 and 22) to make sure you make the most of the capital.

Puerto de Mogán This surely wins the vote for the most attractive – and glamorous – resort on the island (page 42).

Visit a theme park There is a huge selection of theme parks, mostly in the south of the island, which offer entertainment for all the family. You can:
- watch a shoot-out at Sioux City (page 70)
- have fun in the water at Aqualand or Ocean Park (page 73)
- see a huge variety of parrots in the beautiful Palmitos Park (page 68)

- learn about the lifestyle of the island's original inhabitants at Mundo Aborigen (page 59)
- count endless crocodiles at the Parque de Cocodrilo (page 70)
- see donkeys, camels and goats in exotic surrounds at Banana Park (page 70).

A good night out There is plenty of nightlife around in the major resorts, but for that special night, why not:
- catch a show at a casino, either in Las Palmas (page 21) or in San Agustín (page 37)
- enjoy barbecue night at Sioux City, and a 'Wild West' show (page 70).

Visit Teror The old capital (page 54) has fine Canarian wooden balconies and a famous church, Basilica de Señora del Pino.

Tour the mountainous interior The high mountains (page 61) offer spectacular scenery unique to the island. Once you have visited the landmarks of Roque Nublo and Roque Bentayga, you will be able to recognize them from almost anywhere on the island.

Camel trekking No one should leave Gran Canaria without experiencing a camel ride (page 73). There are some great opportunities on this island, and you can trek over sand or ride out to lunch.

Top museums
- The Casa de Colón, Las Palmas (page 15), has exhibits commemorating the visit of Christopher Columbus to the island
- The Museo Canario, Las Palmas (page 17), has a fascinating collection of Aborigen mummies, skulls and other archaeological remains
- The Casa Museo Patronas de la Virgin, in Teror (page 54), is a 17th-century manor house kept intact as a museum; see how an aristocratic family lived in the past.

RESORTS
Places under the sun

Historic Las Palmas
city of contrasts

Compact and atmospheric, the Vegueta quarter is where Las Palmas was founded in 1478. Narrow streets overhung with Canarian balconies, the oldest market and the best museums on the island all await discovery. By contrast, the adjoining 16th-century Triana quarter has one of the best shopping streets in the city and a pleasant park.

Allow half a day for this short walk in order to absorb everything of interest along the way. Use the underpass from the bus station to reach Parque de San Telmo. Columbus himself probably set foot on Gran Canaria at this very location, the site of the original port.

Enjoy a coffee in the park at the exquisitely colourful **Kiosk** before making a foray along pedestrianized Calle Mayor de Triana (see Tips box, page 19). Take the left fork at the bottom and cross the busy road, the boundary between Triana and Vegueta, into Mendizábal. Pop into the **Mercado Municipal**, open from 08.30 to 13.00 hours, to check out the local produce, turning right up Calle de los Balcones towards the rear of the **cathedral** and **Museo de Arta Sacro**.

Admire the typical Canarian balconies and – if the door is open – take a peek into the old courtyard of number 15, just past the **Atlantic Centre of Modern Art**, or **CAAM**. At the top of this Calle, the **Casa de Colón's** imposing facade comes into view, its entrance to be found off narrow Calle Colón.

Continue up the right-hand side of the cathedral and bear left into the Plaza de Santa Ana. Check out the town hall here and the bronze dogs in front of the **Catedral de Santa Ana**, which gave the Canary Islands their name (*canis* is Latin for 'dog'). The route leads to Calle Doctor Chil and a right turn to number 25, the **Museo Canario**.

 Do your shopping in the morning, since many shops in Triana close in the afternoon, and save the museums for later.

THINGS TO SEE & DO

Casa de Colón (Columbus Museum) ★★★

Here is an opportunity to view the inside of a typical 15th-century Canarian house, built for the island's early governors, where Columbus presented his credentials en route to discovering the New World. On view are exhibits from pre-Columbian America, details about Columbus and his voyages, models of his ships, and displays on the development of the Canaries as a stepping-stone to the New World and the origins and history of the city of Las Palmas. ⓐ Calle de Colón 1 ⓣ 928 31 23 73 ⓕ 928 33 11 56 ⓦ www.cabgc.org/area-cultura ⓛ Open Mon–Fri 09.00–15.00, Sat and Sun 09.00–18.00, closed holidays ⓘ Admission free

Casa Museo Pérez Galdós (Museum House of Pérez Galdós) ★★

The life and work of Canarian-born novelist, playwright and critic, Benito Pérez Galdós, is reflected in his birthplace here. This attractive museum contains exhibits of the author's books, furniture that he designed, and a portrait of him by the artist, Sorolla. Galdos was very anti-establishment, and branded as a 'rabid anticleric' – a visit to his home would have been looked on as a mortal sin. ⓐ Calle Cano 6 ⓣ 928 36 69 76 ⓦ www.culturacanaria.com ⓛ Open Mon–Fri 09.00–21.00, Sat 09.00–18.00, closed Sun ⓘ Admission and tour, free

ⓥ *Columbus Museum*

Catedral de Santa Ana (Saint Ana's Cathedral) ★★★

Work began on the cathedral of Santa Ana in 1497, and 70 years later, it continues still. As a result, it is a fascinating mixture of styles, combining a late-Gothic interior and neo-classical exterior. The cathedral contains a fine collection of works of art, including a painting of Christ by Luján Pérez. It can be reached through the Museo Diocesano de Arte Sacro (Diocesan Museum of Sacred Art), but for many visitors, it is enough to sit in the Plaza de Santa Ana and relax. **Cathedral** 🅰 Plaza Santa Ana 🛈 928 33 14 30 Ⓦ www.aruqa.com Ⓛ Open Mon–Sat during service hours, closed Sun ❗ Moderate entry fee

Centro Atlántico de Arte Moderno – CAAM (Atlantic Centre of Modern Art) ★★

This beautifully converted white building on the road behind the Catedral de Santa Ana, is the work of architect Francisco Sáinz de Oiza. He has created a well-balanced modern art gallery behind an 18th-century neo-classical facade. Opened in 1989, it houses the work of contemporary artists, mainly Canarian and Spanish, and is one of the city's main arts centres. 🅰 Calle de los Balcones 8–12 🛈 928 31 80 76/902 31 18 24 🛈 928 32 16 29 Ⓦ www.caam.net Ⓛ Open Mon–Sat 10.00–21.00, Sun 10.00–14.00 ❗ Admission free

🔽 *Catedral de Santa Ana in Plaza Santa Ana*

Ermita de San Antonio Abad (Saint Antonio Abad Chapel) ★★

This 18th-century baroque church stands on the site of Las Palmas's first church, where Columbus is said to have attended Mass before setting off. ❷ Vegueta Quarter, behind Casa de Colón ❶ 928 67 65 99 ❶ Entry needs permission from the Cathequist Institute in Dolores Sopeña

Ermita de San Telmo (Saint Telmo Chapel) ★★

In the Parque de San Telmo, this Canarian church, dedicated to the patron saint of fishermen, was rebuilt in the 17th century following damage by Dutch pirates; the interior is particularly splendid. ❷ In the Parque de San Telmo, corner of Calle Bravo Murillo and Avenida Rafael Cabrera ❶ 928 36 79 70 ❸ Open 09.00–13.00 and 17.00–20.00

Jardín Botánico Canario (Canarian Botanic Garden) ★★★

To learn more about the wide variety of flora growing on Gran Canaria, it is essential to visit this outstanding botanical garden in the Guiniguada *barranco* (gully) at Tafira Baja. The garden was opened in 1952, and houses many plant species endemic to the island. There are entrances at the top and bottom of the *barranco*, with connecting paths that see you past Canarian palms, some of the ancient trees – the laurasilva – that once covered the whole island, and the cactus house, which contains specimens from all over the world. It's a long climb to the top, and a circular viewing point; suitable refreshment is available in a restaurant beside the top entrance. ❷ Tafira Baja is 8 km (5 miles) south of Las Palmas ❶ 928 35 46 13 ❸ Open 09.00–18.00, except 1 January and Good Friday ❶ Admission free

Museo Canario (Canarian Museum) ★★★

This intriguing collection includes items related to the island's geology. Children will be enthralled by the skulls and mummies, as well as illuminated scale models of cave life that create a fascinating picture of the life of the Aborigens, the original inhabitants of the island. ❷ Calle Doctor Chil 25 ❶ 928 33 68 00 ❸ Open Mon–Fri 10.00–20.00, Sat and Sun 10.00–14.00 ❶ Modest entry fee

Museo Néstor (Néstor Museum) ★★

This museum houses the life's work of the island's most famous painter, Néstor Martín Fernández de la Torre (1887–1938), who was particularly incensed by the effect of modern development on the island, but had sound ideas for retaining the best of the traditional Canarian culture and architecture. There is folklore dancing here, Sundays 11.00–noon.
ⓐ Pueblo Canario, on the edge of the Parque Doramas, near the tourist information office ① 928 24 51 35 ① 928 24 35 76 ② Open Tues–Sat 10.00–20.00, Sun and public holidays 10.30–14.30 ① Moderate entry fee

Parque Doramas (Doramas Park) ★

Parque Doramas has shaded walks, exuberant fountains and a splendid variety of exotic trees. Doramas, after whom the park was named, was the last Aborigen king of Eastern Gran Canaria. In 1481, he was fatally wounded in single combat. The Spanish and Guanche forces then locked in a brief battle, the last act of armed resistance against the Spaniards. Many of Doramas's followers threw themselves from the cliffs, an event commemorated by a sculpture in the garden of the nearby hotel, the Santa Catalina. ⓐ Ciudad Jardín ① 928 24 51 35 ② Open daily ① Admission free

Pueblo Canario (Canarian Village) ★★

This small group of buildings attempts to preserve and recreate the best of Canarian architecture. Designed by Néstor, the buildings were built after his death by his brother. There is an attractive little courtyard with shops selling handicrafts and musical instruments, where you can sit and have a quiet coffee or a bite to eat. ⓐ The edge of Parque Doramas

Teatro Pérez Galdós (Pérez Galdós Theatre) ★

This imposing building was designed by architect Miguel Martín Fernández de la Torre. When first publicized, the new building plans were considered too radical, shocking the island's more conservative theatre-goers. It is now a favourite venue for many of the Las Palmas well-to-do. ⓐ Lentini 1, beside one of the main roads between Triana and Vegueta

Vegueta quarter ★★★

Vegueta is the oldest part of Las Palmas, where the Castilian invaders landed in the 15th century, and so it became the powerbase for the ruling classes. It still has a mildly aristocratic air, and contains a number of 17th- and 18th-century mansions with superbly crafted balconies. An unplanned stroll through this part of historic Las Palmas is well worthwhile.

Shopping bargains – main shopping area

Maya The place to go for duty-free electrical or photographic equipment. ● Calle Mayor de Triana 105–107 ● Open daily

El Corte Inglés A department store where there is no bargaining, just genuine goods at good-value prices (see page 25).

RESTAURANTS (see map on page 20)

There are many restaurants and cafés in Las Palmas, and tapas bars abound in the narrow side streets just off and north of the Calle Mayor de Triana. Take your time and wander around, but it is a good idea to book if you are looking for that pricier, intimate dinner for two.

 Café del Real €–€€ ❶ Very pleasant for lunch, tapas, snacks and drinks, with an excellent set lunch. ● Calle Doctor Chil
● Open 08.00–21.00

 Canguro (Kangaroo) € ❷ Convenient for good-value snacks and cakes ● Juan de Quesada ● Open 07.00–21.00

 Casa Montesdeoca €€€ ❸ This expensive, elegant restaurant in a restored mansion has all the atmosphere, service and food you could hope for in such a charming setting. ● Calle Montesdeoca 10
● 928 33 34 66 ● Mon–Sat 12 30–16.00 and 20.00–midnight

 La Casita €€€ ❹ Catering for discerning foodies and lovers of good wine. ● Calle León y Castillo 227, on the edge of the Parque Doramas ● 928 24 54 64 ● 928 23 46 99 ● Open Mon–Sat

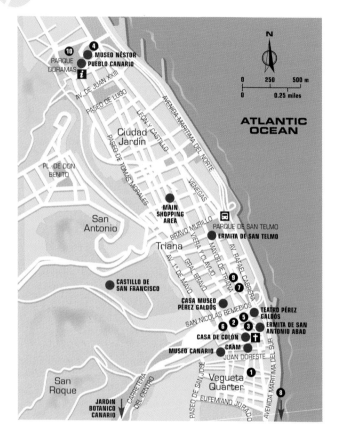

El Herreño €€ **⑤** In this popular, old-town restaurant near the Teatro Pérez Galdós, you will find a good selection of tapas, as well as wines from the furthest south-west Canarian island of El Hierro. ⓐ Calle Mendizábal 5–7 ❶ 928 31 05 13/32 20 40 ⓛ Open 09.30–01.30

🍴 **Hipócrates** €–€€ **⑥** A vegetarian pub-restaurant. ⓐ Calle Colón 4 ☎ 928 31 11 71 🕐 Open Mon 20.30–midnight, Tues–Sat noon–16.00 and 20.30–midnight, Sun noon–1600

🍴 **Koala Restaurant/Café** € **⑦** Sit at the outside tables, enjoying a good range of dishes and drinks, and watch the world go by. ⓐ Calle Mayor de Triana 🕐 Open Mon–Sat 08.30–21.00, Sun 08.30–18.00

🍴 **El Pescador** €€ **⑧** With sea views, this fresh fish restaurant is worthwhile. ⓐ Estribor, Esplanade de Muelle San Cristobal ☎ 928 33 56 61 🕐 Open Mon–Thur noon–17.00 and 19.30–midnight, Fri and Sat noon–17.00 and 19.30–00.30, Sun noon–17.00 ❶ Parking area

 Solo Café € **⑨** Ideal for a coffee stop on the move. Good coffee, low prices and clean toilets. ⓐ Calle Mayor de Triana 🕐 Open Mon–Sat 08.30–21.00, Sun 08.30–18.00

> El Monte, produced south of Las Palmas, may not rival classic Spanish wines, but it has a refreshing, agreeable earthiness.

NIGHTLIFE

No one is overlooked in the night scene of Las Palmas. Parque Santa Catalina is closest to the action, especially that of a more risqué nature, while for the clubbing scene, it's best to seek out posters around the town to find out what is going on, and where. The vogue places are in the Las Arenas Centro Comercial and around the marina, but don't expect too much before 22.00 hours, or to finish before daybreak.

Gran Casino de Las Palmas **⑩** Sophisticated casino, with French/American Roulette, Black Jack and slot machines, and an international restaurant. ⓐ Hotel Santa Catalina, Doramas Park ☎ 928 23 27 91 🕐 Open Mon–Thur 20.00–04.00, Fri and Sat 20.00–05.00, closed Sun; restaurant open 21.00–02.00 ❶ Men are obliged to wear a jacket and tie and your passport is required for entry

Modern Las Palmas
cafés, shopping and more

Shopaholics should head for the Alcaravanera and Santa Catalina quarters of Las Palmas for a sample of just about every shopping experience going. When you reach dropping point, rest at an outside café in Parque Santa Catalina or unwind on the spectacular beach at Playa de las Canteras.

● *The church of San Juan Batista*

Mesa y López is the hub of a major shopping area where large department stores, including **Marks & Spencer**, rub shoulders with cosmopolitan boutiques, such as **Springfields**, **Bounty**, **Globe** and **Zara**, all flaunting the latest adult fashions. Even infant followers of fashion might be tempted into **OshKosh B'gosh**. Shoe shops, such as **López**, abound and walkers will find **Koronel Tapiocca** a real mecca for walking equipment.

Prominent amongst the department stores is **El Corte Inglés**, two stores on opposite sides of the road. The store on the north side concentrates on fashions, whilst the store opposite, in front of the market, sells stationery, books, textiles, electrical goods and photographic equipment. Well worth a quick look is the *mercado* (market), where you can check out the fresh local produce and maybe stock up on some fruit at local prices. Try a *churros con chocolate* at **La Habana** on Calle de Barcelona, on the south side of the market (see Tip box, below). A short walk leads to the Parque Santa Caterina, where there is a tourist information office open Monday to Friday from 09.00 to 14.00 hours, as well as more shops and cafés. Playa de las Canteras beach lies only a short distance beyond.

Start the day as many Canarians do, with a *churros con chocolate* (pronounced 'chooros con choco-lah-tay'). This scrumptious sausage-like whirl of fried batter is broken into chunks and dipped into a glass of thick, hot drinking chocolate. Be warned, though – this addictive delight is usually only available before 11.00 hours.

THINGS TO SEE & DO
Castillo de la Luz (Castle of Light) ★
At the entrance to the Puerto de la Luz, this large fort was built in the 15th century to defend the bay against pirates.

Parque Santa Catalina (Saint Catalina Park) ★★
Apart from its shady trees and flower beds, this park hosts the Rastro, a huge Sunday flea market, from 09.00 to 14.30 hours, where just about everything is sold. A small concert band plays in the square at lunchtime on Sundays.

BEACHES
Playa de las Canteras ★★★
Close to Parque Santa Catalina, and well supplied with facilities for the visitor, this magnificent strand of golden sand stretches for over 3 km (2 miles). A wide, pedestrianized promenade fringes the beach, a popular playground for the locals and for Spaniards from the mainland. At the western end of the beach is **Las Arenas (The Sands)** – yet another shopping centre. 🕐 Open Mon–Sat 10.00–22.00, Sun and holidays 11.00–14.00

EXCURSIONS
Arucas ★★
This town has been busy making rum ever since sugar cane was introduced to the islands. *Ron Arucas*, as it is known, is widely available, but why not slip into a bar here and try one with a coffee? The town is dominated by the huge church of San Juan Batista, easily the finest piece of architecture on the island, with magnificent stained-glass windows.

Firgas ★★
Famous for its spring water, which is bottled and sold all over the island, Firgas even has water cascading down the main street over a series of steps. Equally interesting is the street above, where each of the major islands of the Canaries is represented as a pictorial plaque in colourful tiles, complete with a map in relief.

Puerto de las Nieves ★
Here, you can view the famous 'Finger of God', a slender column of rock just offshore. Viewed across a small beach of black sand, it merges against the black cliffs and cannot always be seen instantly.

Sardina del Norte ★
This small fishing port is probably the most attractive of the few resorts on the north coast. It has a small beach of dark-grey sand and a good selection of bars and restaurants. On a clear day, there is a good view of Tenerife in the distance.

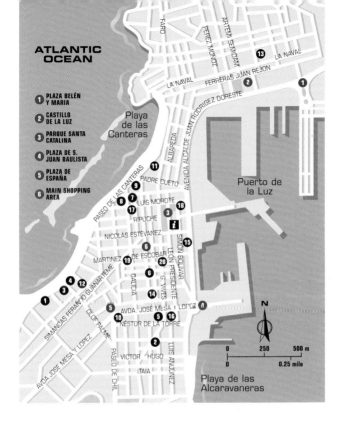

RESTAURANTS (see map, above)

Casa Carmelo €€€ ❶ Expensive, but very friendly atmosphere. Excels in grilled meat, or you can choose your own fish. ⓐ Paseo de las Canteras 2 ☎ 928 46 90 56

La Casa Vasca €€€ ❷ A chance to sample Basque food at its best. This restaurant is expensive, but you won't come here if you are going to worry about that; this is for people who enjoy their food and wine. ⓐ Avenida Alcalde Ramirez Betencour ☎ 928 24 18 29 ⏱ Open Mon–Sat, closed Sun and hols

El Cerdo Que Rie € ❸ Inexpensive grill parlour; good food, which includes flambéed dishes and fondues. Ⓐ Paseo de las Canteras 31 Ⓣ 928 26 36 49

Chino House €€ ❹ Mainly Cantonese food at this reasonably priced eatery, between historic and modern Las Palmas, over-looking Playa de las Canteras. Ⓐ Paseo de las Canteras 30

El Corte Inglés €–€€€ ❺ A lunchtime restaurant in this very prestigious department store. Most dishes are international cuisine, though there is a good selection of Spanish dishes. Ⓐ Avenida José Mesa y López 18 Ⓣ 928 26 30 00 Ⓛ Closed evenings

Don Quijote I €€ ❻ You may be forgiven for expecting Spanish food here, but the menu is largely Belgian dishes; ideal for those who enjoy a good steak. Ⓐ Calle Secretario Artiles Ⓣ 928 27 27 86

Frogy's € ❼ Fast food, offering breakfast, and sandwiches. Ⓐ Plaza Miguel Martin

El Gallo Feliz (The Happy Cockerel) €€ ❽ Wide selection of dishes. Ⓐ Paseo de las Canteras 35 Ⓣ 928 27 17 31

Heladaria € ❾ Ice-cream parlour with a wide range of flavours. Ⓐ Paseo de las Canteras 31

McDonald's € ❿ Ⓐ Corner of Jósé Mesa y López with Plaza de España and on the beachfront at the Paseo de las Canteras

Al Maccaroni € ⓫ Try this restaurant for Italian pizzas, pasta, fish and meat dishes Ⓐ Paseo de las Canteras 12 Ⓣ 928 27 15 80 Ⓘ Free parking available

El Novillo Precoz €€€ **12** This place specializes in steak, with beef apparently flown in almost daily from Uruguay! Expensive, but wonderful. 🅐 Calle Portugal 9 📞 928 22 16 59/26 54 02

Restaurante Casa Julio €€ **13** This restaurant offers a range of fish and seafood dishes. But the chef knows his way around roast and grilled meats, too, and there is also a selection of typical Canarian dishes. 🅐 Calle la Naval 132 📞 928 46 01 39 🕐 Open Mon–Sat

De Tapa en Tapa € **14** Good for a light meal or snack. 🅐 Corner of Juan Manuel Durán and Diderot 23 📞 928 49 00 55

Tony Roma's €–€€ **15** American chain restaurant famous for its ribs 🅐 Calle Simón Bolivar 📞 928 22 64 00 📠 928 26 29 02

NIGHTLIFE

Cuasquias **16** Smart and ideal venue for all ages. Good Latin American music and top jazz. 🅐 Calle San Pedro 2 📞 928 38 38 40

Neon Dancing **17** Dancing to an old-fashioned orchestra. 🅐 Calle Luis Morote 61 📞 928 26 60 79 🕐 Open 21.00–03.00

Pacha Las Palmas **18** A good all-night disco. 🅐 Simon Bolivar 3 📞 928 27 16 84 🕐 Open 23.00, closed Sun

Sheehan's **19** A bustling Irish pub. 🅐 Los Martinez de Escobar 8 📞 928 26 07 29

El Tren **20** A live music bar for a wide range of ages. 🅐 Calle Domingo de Navarro 19 🕐 Open Mon–Thur from 21.00, Fri and Sat from 22.00, closed Sun

Playa del Inglés
Gran Canaria's premier resort

This is where it's at, the place that buzzes through the night, that never seems to want to rest, and that is undoubtedly the island's premier resort. Almost surrounded by sand, it has everything a visitor could wish for. It is well served by public transport, and taxis and car-hire firms are legion. Although there is no obvious centre – no tree-shaded plaza such as you might find in Las Palmas, for example – there is nevertheless a throbbing vibrancy about El Inglés, as it is also known, that more than compensates.

Everything happens in or around the numerous commercial centres (*centros comerciales*), which in the evening become lively, animated haunts for disco fanatics, the gay and lesbian community and party-goers.

🔺 *Sun, sand and sea*

Here, sunshine is virtually guaranteed, the beach, which seems to go on forever, is splendid, and the range of its facilities and services are second to none. There's even an **Internet Club**, on Avenida de Gran Canaria, for those who want to keep in touch with home.

The nearest thing to a town centre is the sprawling complex of the **Yumbo Centrum**, close by the main tourist office, on Avenida de Estados Unidos. The Yumbo is the largest of just one of 14 similar centres in El Inglés, all of them vast bazaars of clothes, leather and electronic goods, perfume and souvenirs. And, if you have the time to slip away from the centre for a while, the **San Fernando market** (see below) is by far the largest on the island.

But in the evening, as the temperature drops, the place to be, before heading for the discos, bars and restaurants, is the promenade along the coast, the **Paseo Costa Canaria**, which extends from the beach at San Agustin to Maspalomas and then continues from Maspalomas to Pasito Blanco – not that you need to walk from end to end!

THINGS TO SEE & DO
Mini Tren ★
Ride this miniature train, which takes a circular route through town from the El Veril Centre in Avenida de Italia.

Perla Canaria (Canary Pearl) ★
Take a trip to Perla Canaria, where you can choose your own pearls from the oyster tank, and witness the skill of pearl threading. There is a licenced café and a children's play area. ➋ On the road to Palmitos Park, bus no. 45 runs every 15 min from Playa, bus no. 70 runs every 30 min from Puerto Rico ☎ 928 14 14 64 🕒 Open 09.00–19.30 ❶ Free parking, and facilities for visitors with disabilities

San Fernando market ★★
Quite apart from the shopping centres (see page 33), the market (mercado) in Playa del Inglés is the largest on the island, and well worth a visit. 🕒 Open Wed and Sat 08.30–13.00

Drinks and ice cream are much cheaper at bars and shops away from the promenade.

RESTAURANTS (see map, opposite)

Casa Vieja €€ **①** This is one of the few typically Canarian restaurants in the resort and it is particularly popular at lunchtime. It has a good atmosphere in the evenings, when the guitarists are busy serenading diners. The menu is well balanced between fish and meat. Why not finish with fresh papaya in liqueur? ⓐ Calle de Fataga 139, San Fernando ❶ 928 76 90 10

Chipi-Chipi €–€€ **②** Good food, well presented. ⓐ Edificio Barbados 1, Avenida de Tirajana ❶ 928 76 50 88

Las Cumbres €€ **③** Typical Spanish restaurant, with roast lamb as a tasty speciality. ⓐ Avenida de Tirajana 11 ❶ 928 76 09 41

Harley Rock Café €–€€ **④** Inexpensive American diner where you can drop in for a jailhouse burger or pork ribs and finish with home-made apple pie in a friendly and buzzing atmosphere. ⓐ Apartments Koka, Avenida de Tenerife 17 ❶ 928 77 09 28

El Portalón €€€ **⑤** A smart restaurant with good meat and fish cuisine, and an impressive wine list. ⓐ Avenida de Tirajana 27 ❶ 928 77 16 22

Rias Bajas €€€ **⑥** A chance to dine in elegant surroundings in one of the more expensive restaurants. Choose from a full international menu or select your own fresh fish from the display in the refrigerated cabinet. ⓐ Edificio Playa del Sol, Avenida de Tirajana ❶ 928 76 40 33/85 48

La Toja €€ **⑦** Outstanding fish restaurant. Try *calde de pescado*, fish and vegetable soup. ⓐ Avenida de Tirajana 17 ❶ 928 76 11 96

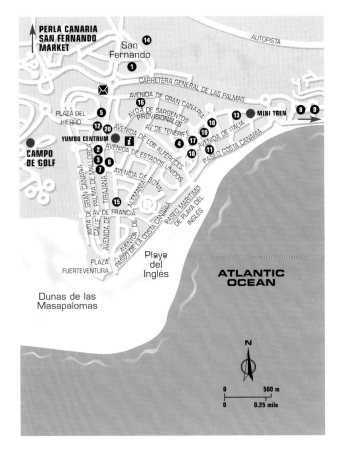

Toro Negro II €€ €€€ ❶ Excellent restaurant overlooking the sea, which serves a very good menu at extremely reasonable prices. ❸ Centro Comercial Tropical 14 (near the Hotel Tropical) ❶ 928 76 67 40

⬥ *Playa del Inglés*

NIGHTLIFE

Casino Palace ❾ Take in dinner and a show at the casino. ⓐ Calle las Retamas 3 ☎ 928 77 40 90 ⏰ Open from 19.30, winter only

Discoteca Joy ❿ Trendy disco for the under-30s wanting to party the night away. ⓐ Avenida de Gran Canaria ☎ 928 76 23 99 ⏰ 23.00–06.00

Pachà Playa del Inglés ⓫ Great club, from the same company as the Las Palmas original. ⓐ Avenida Sargentos Provisionales 10 ☎ 928 76 92 01

Playa del Sol ⓬ Dance the night away to top disco music; includes TV bar with all English channels ⓐ Avda de Tirajana ⏰ Open 20.00–02.00

SHOPPING

 This resort's shopping centres seem to have it all, with restaurants and bars, live singers, karaoke and plenty of shops. Here are some of the main centres:

Aguila Roja ⓭ This is the home of several Irish bars and restaurants serving good Irish food. There is plenty of live music around and there are a few gift shops to fill in spare moments.

Bella Vista ⓮ A new commercial centre located behind the Ansoco supermarket in San Fernando.

Cita ⓯ One of the largest, with excellent duty-free shopping, supermarkets and plenty of souvenir shops.

Gran Chapparal ⓰ For a good pub, this is the place to start. Decent British food is also on offer in the bars and restaurants. Satellite television offering live football is a major attraction.

Kasba ⓱ Has the reputation of being the liveliest at night, with many busy bars and restaurants. It is also a good place to buy leather goods, ceramics, duty-free goods and perfumes.

Metro ⓲ Extending to four floors, with a great choice of bars and snack bars scattered amongst the many shops.

Plaza Maspalomas ⓳ A touch upmarket, with designer clothes, shoe shops, jewellery and perfumeries.

Yumbo ⓴ This centre is home to the Mardi Gras festival every March. Bars and restaurants here are especially popular with the gay community. Shop here for leather and electrical goods, and souvenirs.

San Agustín
the ideal place to unwind

Strangely, this resort, only a short distance away from the action in Playa del Inglés, has never experienced the same mass tourism invasion, and has managed, quite successfully, to maintain an upmarket image. This contrast is highlighted by the fact that it is home to some of the island's most prestigious hotels, including the Melia Tamarindos and its casino. In winter, the resort is host to the famous and erotic Casino Palace Show (see page 37).

The resort is in two halves, separated by the no. 812 highway, and connected by a series of pedestrian footbridges. Further east is the small resort of Bahía Feliz, a new development of modern bungalows and apartment hotels specifically designed with young, dynamic and well-off clientele in mind.

BEACHES

The main beach, of dark sand, is the **Playa de San Agustín**, with smaller beaches, the **Playa del Morro Besudo** and the **Playa de las Burras**, on either side. These are the first of the south-coast beaches, and the sands stretch all the way beyond Playa del Inglés to Maspalomas. Sunbeds and parasols can be hired for the day, but there are no water sports here, which means that by comparison it is much quieter and more relaxed. Beachfront cafés along the Playa de las Burras make this the perfect place for the less energetic holidaymaker.

THINGS TO SEE & DO
Diving ★★

Daily diving tuition and underwater trips, and some night dives. Transport to and from your hotel and all equipment and insurance is included in the price – **Padi Diving School/Nordic Divers** @ Based at the Aeroclub on the GC1 motorway, exit at Tarajalillo, near Bahía Feliz
☎ 660 29 18 91

Flying ★★★

Just a short distance north east of San Agustín is the **Real Aero Club de Gran Canaria**, which offers tandem parachute jumps over the Maspalomas dunes. There is also a good restaurant here ☎ 928 15 71 03. This exhilarating way of seeing the coastline is not for the faint-hearted. You can also book flying lessons here or learn how to free-fall. ➌ Carretera General del Sur ☎ 928 15 71 47 ◷ Open Wed–Mon, by appointment

Go-karting ★★★

The **Gran Karting Club** is the largest in Spain. It provides an ideal variation to the diet of sun, sand and sea. ➌ Carretera General del Sur ☎ 928 15 71 90 ☎ 928 29 36 71 ◷ Open 11.00–22.00 (summer); 10.00–21.00 (winter)

Sioux City ★★★

This Wild West Show, with jail-breaks, shoot-outs, and bows and arrows, is tremendously popular with children (see page 70).

Water Therapy Centre ★★★

This spa is for those of us who love to pamper ourselves. Shouldn't be missed, but not for children. ➌ Gloria Palace Hotel in San Agustín ☎ 928 76 56 89/77 64 04 ☎ 928 76 57 46 ⓦ www.hotelgloriapalace.com

RESTAURANTS & BARS (see map on page 36)

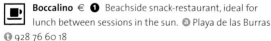

Boccalino € ❶ Beachside snack-restaurant, ideal for lunch between sessions in the sun. ➌ Playa de las Burras ☎ 928 76 60 18

Chino Canton €€ ❷ Excellent-value Cantonese-style cuisine served in comfortable surroundings. Peking duck has to be ordered 24 hours in advance. ➌ Calle de las Aulagas ☎ 928 76 62 30

Don Quijote € ❸ Panoramic day- and night-time views over San Agustín from this rooftop bar. ➌ Top floor, Commercial Centre

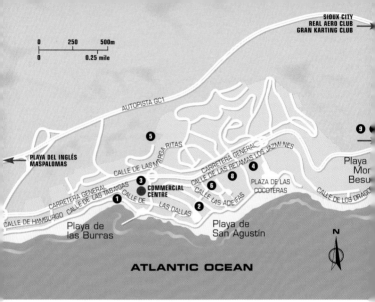

Drago's Bar €€–€€€ **④** Upmarket cocktail bar within the elegant Hotel Melia Tamarindos. In the winter months, the Casino Palace Singers sometimes entertain. **ⓐ** Calle de las Retamas

La Gorbea €€€ **⑤** Elegant restaurant with spectacular panoramic views. Treat yourself to goose liver pâté, sole with champagne sauce or Chateaubriand. **ⓐ** Top floor, Gloria Palace Hotel **ⓣ** 928 12 85 00/902 26 86 03

Loopys €€ **⑥** Sits on a corner where customers can relax and watch the world go by from the terrace area. Specializes in steaks and pizzas, plus kebabs and Beef Stroganoff. Excellent value and a friendly atmosphere. **ⓐ** Calle de las Retamas Los Jazmines **ⓣ** 928 76 28 92 **ⓦ** www.loopysonline.com

The Old Gramophone €–€€ **③** Cosy and intimate piano bar, perfect for a late nightcap. **ⓐ** Ground floor, Commercial Centre

Restaurante Los Pescadores €€ ❼ Fresh fish and seafood restaurant, good value for money. ⓐ Calle Esquina Bahía Feliz ⓣ 928 15 71 79 ⓛ Closed on Wed

Riverboat €€ ❸ Provides a relaxed holiday atmosphere for country-and-western fans, with live music from guest bands, and karaoke. ⓐ Ground Floor, Commercial Centre

Tony's Bar-Grill €–€€ ❸ This restaurant offers a varied menu with excellent quality and prices. ⓐ Second floor, Commercial Centre

NIGHTLIFE

Casino ❽ Guests are free to try their luck at the One-Armed Bandits or attempt to become a millionaire on the Blackjack or roulette tables. Alternatively, you can sit back and watch from the comfort of the Casino Bar. Or you can go to the **Casino Palace Show**, located within the casino itself, and one of the highlights of the winter months, incorporating the beauty of the Spanish Ballet, the fun and laughter of magicians and comedians, and the dynamic dance routines of the Casino Palace Dancers. ⓣ 928 77 40 90 (reception) ⓐ Calle de las Retamas ⓛ Casino open all year round; show runs Nov–Apr ⓘ Small admission charge

Garbo's Dinner Show ❾ For an excellent night out, try this place. ⓐ Ctra General del Sur Bahia Feliz ⓣ 928 15 70 60 ⓕ 928 15 70 99 ⓛ Open 19.30–midnight

SHOPPING

All the shops are to be found in the Commercial Centre, where you will find a good selection of leather goods, perfumes and other cosmetics and gift items.

Maspalomas
Saharan sand dunes

Lying adjacent to Playa del Inglés, Maspalomas is separated from its neighbour only by an extensive system of Sahara-like sand dunes. It is much quieter in character than Playa del Inglés, but boasts a good selection of bars and restaurants. Life revolves around the beach and surrounding shops by day, and includes the Faro 2 shopping centre at night. Visitors looking for a nightlife buzz mostly travel into Playa del Inglés.

This is a great place for lazy days on the beach, a major feature in this resort. It extends eastwards, first to the lagoon, fringed with grasses, and beyond to the extensive sand dunes. These are a great playground in themselves and are a protected area. Behind part of the beach lies the Paseo de Faro, full of bars, cafés and souvenir shops, where you can catch anything from a cool beer or a light snack to a full meal.

The **Faro**, or lighthouse, is a significant landmark lying on the western side of the resort. Further west lies another beach, the **Playa de la Mujer**. This beach occupies a corner too breezy for sunbathers, but the rough seas and windy conditions are favoured by board and windsurfers.

Further west still is **Pasito Blanco**; accessible from the main highway, the public may walk down to this small, private spot. It provides access to the more sheltered end of the Playa de la Mujer, where those who seek a little peace and quiet in order to sunbathe nude may find it.

Inland from Pasito Blanco, off to the right on the GC812 going from Maspalomas to Mogán, is a recently opened outdoor activity club, for trekking and mountain bike rental, but only for organized groups.

Two 18-hole golf courses are worth visiting in the area: the new **Salobre Golf** ✆ 928 01 01 03/828 06 18 28 📠 928 01 01 04/828 06 18 29 ✉ reservation@salobregolfresort.com ⊕ www.salobregolfresort.com; and lying behind the sand dunes is the excellent **Campo de Golf**. The restaurant overlooking the course is open to the general public (see Restaurants & Bars, page 41).

THINGS TO SEE & DO
Camel riding in the dunes ★ ★ ★

Take a camel trek through the famous Maspalomas dunes and imagine you are in the Sahara. Make it into a special occasion by continuing on to the **Rancho Verde** for an Arabian meal followed by a belly-dancing show. ❶ 928 76 07 81 (office) ❶ 928 14 02 05 (ranch) ❶ Be sure to book ahead

Dune trekking ★

It is easier to walk back from Playa del Inglés to Maspalomas, using the Faro as a guide, than the other way round. From the end of the access road through the Riu Palace Hotel, at the end of Avenida de Tirajana in Playa del Inglés, it is possible to see the Faro in Maspalomas. Use it to navigate by as you trek, like Lawrence of Arabia, across the dunes – not recommended after a late night in a bar, but good for some stimulating exercise the next day. Walking across sand is far from easy and will give you aching calves – allow an hour and 30 minutes for the walk.

⬇ *The dunes of Maspalomas*

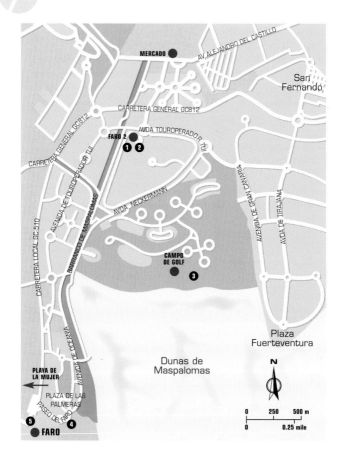

Sky diving ★★★

A 20-min flight over Gran Canaria, then free falling for 45 seconds before opening your parachute. ☎ 928 157325 ⓦ www.skydivegrancanaria.es; or try, **Jump the Beach** ☎ 928 15 70 00 ⓔ info@jump-for-life.com

RESTAURANTS & BARS (see map, opposite)

Altstadt Düsseldorf €€ ❶ Offering excellent views, with a full international menu. After a shrimps-in-garlic starter, you coud try the Chateaubriand. ⓐ Upper floor, Faro 2 Commercial Centre

Broncemar 2 €€ ❷ This restaurant is especially famous for its steaks, but you can just as easily choose the grilled lobster from the seafood section or the chicken from the general list.
ⓐ Ground floor, Faro 2 Commercial Centre ❶ 928 76 89 87
🕐 Open 10.00–23.00

Campo de Golf €€ ❸ Enjoy good views over the fairways in this comfortable but formal atmosphere. The menu is varied, so if the speciality German sausage is not for you, you can select from the pizza list or go for a peppered sirloin. ⓐ Avenida Neckermann ❶ 928 76 87 51

Piano Beach Bar €€ ❹ A very relaxed atmosphere greets visitors to this upmarket bar, where the pianist plays nightly. There is additional entertainment on some nights. ⓐ Paseo del Faro

Restaurante Canton Faro €–€ ❺ Chinese restaurant with good cuisine at excellent value. ⓐ Boulevard El Faro, behind the Hotel Costa Meloneras ❶ 928 14 36 99 🕐 Open noon–23.00

SHOPPING

Arguineguin Market Tuesday is market day in Arguineguin, west of Maspalomas, with souvenirs, T-shirts, clothing, African wood carvings and fresh fruit on offer. The harbour, too, is interesting, especially when freshly caught fish are being unloaded.
Faro 2 Commercial Centre Circular in design and built on two floors, this major attraction has a slightly upmarket air, not only in the style and appearance, but also in the goods on display.

Puerto de Mogán
pretty as a picture

Puerto de Mogán easily wins the accolade of being the most charming port on the island, with the added bonus that a visit here can make you feel like a millionaire. One of the greatest pleasures in this smart marina is spotting luxury yachts and pretending that they belong to you, or trying to guess which rich and famous people they might really belong to.

Unlike most other resorts in the south, Puerto de Mogán has a history, and started out as a fishing village serving the needs of inland Mogán. With the growing demands of tourism, it has developed into a marina – and while the fishermen's cottages have been preserved, they are not in their original form. Now little remains of the old character, and the town has effectively been converted into a model village.

Neat, uniform rows of old cottages now look freshly made from confectioner's icing sugar and as white as the virgin snow. Hand-painted borders around doors and windows – in pastel ochre, deep green or soft purple – make each new house encountered so different from its neighbour. The final drapes of scarlet bougainvillea tumbling from wrought-iron balconies, with borders of peach-coloured hibiscus, create a picture that is as refreshing as it is unexpected. Small, arched bridges, crossing waterways and connecting houses, emphasize the Lilliputian scale and lend the resort a pleasing touch of Venice.

Puerto de Mogán has an atmosphere best enjoyed at leisure. It is a place for strolling, enjoying the marina activities and watching the fishermen arrive with their catch. There are plenty of waterside cafés and bars to sit in while reflecting on life and watching the world at play.

There is no better or more elegant place on the island than Puerto de Mogán to sit and enjoy a sundowner (an alcoholic drink, taken at dusk), and watch the sun set in all its glory.

THINGS TO SEE & DO

Diving aboard the Yellow Submarine ★★

A thrilling trip to the bottom of the sea on the *Yellow Submarine* starts here in Puerto de Mogán. This vessel was commissioned in 1988 and built in Finland especially for observing marine life. The journey beneath the high seas lasts around 45 minutes. There are free buses that depart from many hotels at various times. For more information, ask your representative or at your hotel. ☏ 928 56 51 08   ☏ 928 56 50 48
🕑 The boat departs every 50 minutes, starting at 10.00 hours and ending with the final departure at 17.10 hours

EXCURSIONS

Mogán ★★

Mogán village lies 12 km (7 miles) inland, up one of the most fertile and beautiful valleys on the island. It is easy to head to Mogán for lunch by bus no. 84, but keep an eye on the return times. Riding up the valley, you will pass crops of aubergines, papayas, avocados and coffee beans, which eventually give way to the green pastures of the upper valley. Mogán itself is a small, fairly typical Canarian mountain village that has adapted to greet tourists riding up from the port. Terraces by the church and town hall provide good picnic places. There are some good restaurants lining the main road.

🍴 **El Alamo ❶** (see map, page 44) has a panoramic terrace – try traditional Canarian rabbit or goat in garlic sauce without breaking the bank.

🔺 *Mogán*

BEACHES

There is a good-sized beach of grey sand adjacent to the marina at Puerto de Mogán. The drab colour of the sand makes the beach look uninspiring, but it is as comfortable as any other – although, since dark colours absorb heat, it can get a little hotter in the sun. The beach is well sheltered and there are sunbeds for hire, as well as waterskiing facilities.

Puerto de Mogán to Mogán 10 km

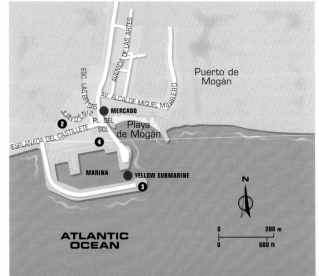

RESTAURANTS (see map opposite)

There are several reasonable places to eat and drink, but most of the restaurants around the harbour are expensive. For better value, at the cost of losing the beautiful views, try to find somewhere away from the harbour front.

El Castillete €€ **❷** This reasonably priced snack bar offers a fairly standard menu at reasonable prices. The lunchtime set menu is good value. ❸ Esplanada del Castillete

El Faro €€€ **❸** This rather expensive restaurant is set around the base of the lighthouse at the end of the harbour quay. The menu is fully international and very extensive. Daytime snacks are also available here at very reasonable prices. ❸ Puerto de Mogán Marina

Meson Patio Canaria 2 €€ CCC **❹** Attractive restaurant with good regional fish dishes. Pricey, but good menu. Try the spiny lobster casserole or grilled stone bass. ❸ Esplanada del Castillete (Patio Canaria) ❶ 928 56 53 69

Tu Casa €€ **❺** Reasonably priced restaurant specializing in fish; try the *parrillada de pescado*. ❸ Puerto de Mogán, in the main square ❶ 928 56 50 78 ❶ Open Wed–Mon

SHOPPING

Friday is market day in Puerto de Mogán, when the large market spreads over vast areas of the car park, the rear of the beach and the adjacent streets. Lace tablecloths, leather goods, clothing, African carvings, and souvenirs can be found in abundance here.

🔺 *Puerto Rico marina*

Puerto Rico
golden sands

Puerto Rico is a compact and picturesque resort, which surrounds a very attractive, family-orientated beach of dark golden sand. There is a good centre for water sports on one side of the beach and a busy marina on the other. The rest of the resort tiers loftily up the hillsides that surround Puerto Rico like an amphitheatre.

BEACHES

The focal point of this resort is the naturally sheltered beach. Further protection is provided by enclosing piers, which calm the seas to make a safe beach for children. It is also great for water sports (see page 48), but these take place outside the bay.

Participants are marshalled in and out and swimmers are protected by a roped-off area. The shallow seas within the bay are greatly enjoyed, particularly by young children. Sun loungers and umbrellas are available for hire, with good drinks and snacks facilities at the rear of the beach.

Although the beach is a good size, it can still be crowded. The pier enclosing the beach on the marina side is lined with sunbeds. It is ideal for those who like to sunbathe without getting sand between the toes. A **rope suspension bridge** over the river here gives public access to Avenida de Muelle Grande and the marina itself.

Bustling at the best of times, this marina is the starting point for a whole variety of sailing excursions. The *Salmon Line* ferry offers regular sailings to neighbouring ports (see page 48), and departs from here.

The rocky coastline between Arguineguin and Puerto de Mogán offers few opportunities to sunbathe, but where it does, new, smaller and decidedly quieter resorts develop. Two such – and definitely worth going that bit further for – are the **Playa de Balito** and the **Playa del Cura**.

Heading 5 km (3 miles) west from Puerto Rico towards Mogán, there is a beautiful, new, man-made beach called **Playa de Amadores**. It is very safe for swimming, and has every amenity: showers, toilets, cafés and restaurants.

SHOPPING

There are two shopping centres in town: the Centro Comercial and the Europa Centre. Plenty of duty-free goods are on offer, including video cameras, electrical goods, perfumes and after-shaves, as well as souvenirs, including the famous Lladró pottery from the Centro Comercial.

THINGS TO SEE & DO

Arguineguin by boat ★★

The *Salmon Line* in Puerto Rico runs trips to Arguineguin for the market. ⓐ Puerto Rico harbour ⓛ First departure is at 10.30, daily, and then every two hours until 16.30

Diving ★★

The Aquanauts Dive Centre offers a chance to descend into a new world, with daily dives. Night dives are also available, plus full-day dives and introductory courses for beginners. ⓐ Puerto Rico harbour ⓣ 928 56 06 55 ⓔ info@aquanauts-divecenter.com

Ferry to Puerto de Mogán ★★★

The *Salmon Line* sails from Puerto Rico harbour to Puerto de Mogán (page 42). ⓣ 928 24 37 08/649 91 93 83/649 92 59 18 ⓛ Sails daily at 10.00 and then hourly until 17.00; return times are 45 minutes later than departure times ⓘ Single or return tickets can be purchased on board for €9 return, or €5.50 single; children up to the age of 10 travel free

Sailing ★★

For anyone who is staying in Puerto Rico for two weeks and whose children have a desire to learn how to sail, the 13-day summer sailing course, the **Escuela de Vela Joaquin Blanco Torrent**, is specifically targeted at 8 to 15-year-olds, and includes theory and practice. Course pupils do get time off for other sports like football and volleyball. ⓐ Calle Olympícos Doreste Y Molina ⓣ 928 56 07 72 ⓛ Bookings can be made via Federación Canaria de la Vela

Taking to the water ★★

Puerto Rico is a great centre for water sports. Here you can paddle out gently on a pedalo; windsurfing is also available and experienced sailors can hire a sailing boat. All these facilities are available from the western side of the beach.

RESTAURANTS (see map, below)

Big Horn Steak House €€–€€€ **1** For something rather more upmarket – but be prepared to pay a little more. It specializes in steak dishes and has a very tempting menu. Children are catered for with their own menu. ⓐ Centro Comercial Puerto Rico ⓣ 928 56 19 03 ⓛ Closed Mon

Los Danieles € **1** This is a much-frequented bar/café, popular with locals and tourists alike. If you want a snack, this is the place to go. ⓐ 3rd fase, Centro Comercial Puerto Rico

Don Quijote €€ **2** This restaurant offers an extensive menu, especially the starters, which include a tapas selection. From frog's legs or buttered French beans with ham, you could move on to quails in red wine or settle for a good steak. The special lunchtime Terrace Menu is very good value. ⓐ Edificio Porto Novo ❶ 928 56 09 01 🕒 Closed 8 Jun–30 Aug

La Habana €€ **1** Tex-Mex food and Latin American music. ⓐ Centro Comercial Puerto Rico

Restaurant El Gaitero €€ **3** On the way into the resort, this first-floor restaurant specializes in regional Galician dishes. Try a genuine *paella Valenciana*. ⓐ Barranco Aqua la Perra ❶ 928 56 20 44

Restaurant Taj Tandoori €–€€ **1** Very good quality, well-priced, Indian food, with English-speaking staff. ⓐ Top floor, 3rd fase, Centro Comercial Puerto Rico, opposite MGM Puerto Rico ❶ 928 72 50 63 🕒 Open 17.00–midnight

The Winston Churchill €€ **1** Caters in British and Indian food, offering good-value meals, from cottage pie and sirloin steaks to balti or tikka masala. Caters well for children. ⓐ Second floor, 3rd fase, Centro Comercial Puerto Rico ❶ 928 56 15 26 🕒 Closed Mon

NIGHTLIFE
Cabaret Night Club Eve **4** A good, nightly disco. ⓐ Calle de Lanzarote 13 ❶ 928 56 17 35 🕒 Open 22.00–05.00

Disco Joker **1** Popular with under 30s. Music from the charts gives way to dance music as the night wears on. ⓐ Basement, Centro Comercial Puerto Rico ❶ 928 72 51 08 🕒 Open 23.00–07.00 ❶ Free before 01.00

EXCURSIONS
Out & about

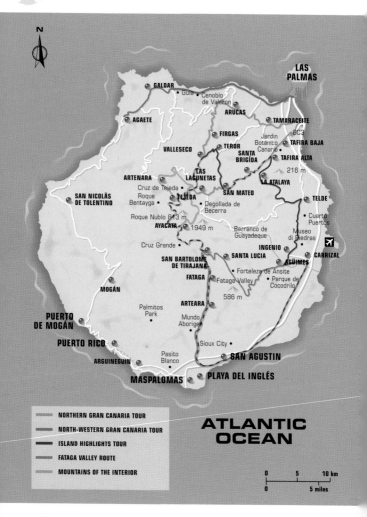

N

LAS PALMAS

GALDAR
Guía • Cenobio de Valerón
AGAETE
ARUCAS
TAMARACEITE
GC3
FIRGAS
Jardin Botánico Canario
TAFIRA BAJA
VALLESECO
TEROR
SANTA BRÍGIDA
TAFIRA ALTA
216 m
ARTENARA
LAS LAGUNETAS
LA ATALAYA
Cruz de Tejeda •
SAN NICOLÁS DE TOLENTINO
Roque Bentayga •
TEJEDA
SAN MATEO
TELDE
Roque Nublo 813 m
• Degollada de Becerra
Cuerto Puertos
AYACATA • 1949 m
Barranco de Guayadeque
Museo di Piedras
Cruz Grande •
INGENIO
CARRIZAL
SANTA LUCÍA
SAN BARTOLOMÉ DE TIRAJANA
• Forteleza de Ansite
AGÜIMES
FATAGA
Fataga Valley
• Parque de Cocodrilo
586 m
MOGÁN
ARTEARA
Palmitos Park
Mundo Aborigen
PUERTO DE MOGÁN
PUERTO RICO
• Sioux City
SAN AGUSTIN
ARGUINEGUIN
Pasito Blanco
MASPALOMAS
PLAYA DEL INGLÉS

ATLANTIC OCEAN

- NORTHERN GRAN CANARIA TOUR
- NORTH-WESTERN GRAN CANARIA TOUR
- ISLAND HIGHLIGHTS TOUR
- FATAGA VALLEY ROUTE
- MOUNTAINS OF THE INTERIOR

| 0 | 5 | 10 km |
| 0 | 5 miles | |

Island highlights tour

This long day trip (192 km/120 miles) offers a rich mix of lowland and mountain scenery with a few well-chosen stopping places, beginning and ending at Playa del Inglés (see page 28).

Consider doing this trip at the weekend, because there is a big local market in Teror, one of the best on the island, which starts up on Saturday and is in full swing by Sunday. Watch out for the special breads on sale here, such as *pan de huevo* (egg bread), *milo* (corn bread), *ajo* (garlic bread) and *leche, pasas y almendras* (milk, raisin and almond bread).

THE ROUTE

Head off in the direction of Las Palmas on the GC1. Leave at the Carrizal junction and take the road to Ingenio. Turn right at the lights in Ingenio on to the unsigned but main road to Telde. Look for the Museo de Piedras on the right very soon after.

Museo de Piedras ★★

The displays here cover a curious mixture of lace, bric-a-brac, Canarian bedroom furniture, rocks and corals, not to mention a small chapel and a parrot in a cage! As much as anything else, it is also a shop, so there is a chance to buy lace (especially tablecloths), leather goods and jewellery.

Further on, just before joining the main road to Telde, is a sign for Cuarto Puertas, an ancient sacred site. Negotiate Telde using the eastern bypass and immediately beyond the last roundabout, turn left to La Atalaya and Caldera Bandama to view the crater.

Caldera Bandama (Bandama Cauldron) ★★

This requires only a brief stop to inspect, and perhaps photograph, the perfectly formed volcanic crater. A farm nestles 200 m (656 ft) down on the bottom, surviving on the fertility of the weathered volcanic soil. The route now leads to Tafira Alta, Santa Brígida and on to San Mateo.

A BITE TO EAT

On the way to Parque Nacional de Tejeda, you pass through Artenara village, which has two great places to eat:

Las Perdiz The owner, Antonio, is very friendly and the menu is varied and good value. ➌ Opposite the petrol station ➊ 928 66 60 71 ➍ Open Tues–Sun noon–late

La Vetetia is also a well-known local meeting place, with good service and a bit of class. It specializes in meat dishes. ➊ 928 66 07 64 ➍ Closed Mon

San Mateo ★★★

There is a good market here on the weekend, where you can buy fresh fruit and vegetables, home-grown herbs and local cheeses and wines.

Teror ★★★

Teror was once the island capital, and architecturally it is the finest Canarian town on the island. Wooden balconies are a feature of old Canarian houses and there are plenty to see in Teror. There is hardly any need to walk further than the street facing the **Basilica de Señora del Pino** to see a good selection.

The basilica is dedicated to the Virgin of the Pines, the patron saint of Gran Canaria. The legend is that, in 1481, the Virgin Mary appeared on the branch of a pine tree before the village priest. A simple church was built on the site in 1515 and there has been a church there ever since. Now greatly modified, the present building has an impressive baroque facade, while inside there is a coffered ceiling and some fine carving. Catching the eye most of all is the richly decorated statue of the Madonna, set in the high altar, sumptuously adorned in gold, silver and precious stones.

Located across the road adjacent to the church entrance is the **Casa Museo Patronas de la Virgin**, a fine old traditional Canarian house belonging to the aristocratic Manrique de la Lara family. It is now open as a museum. The entrance leads first into a shady inner courtyard with fine wooden balconies. From here there is access to the various rooms, all still furnished in the old style. Horse-drawn carriages, sedan chairs and a 1951 Triumph Renown are garaged in the rear courtyard.

Leave Teror on the Firgas road, but climb through Valleseco, eventually reaching Cruz de Tejeda.

● *Typical Canarian wooden balconies*

Cruz de Tejeda & the Roque Nublo ★★★

Located high in the mountains at an altitude of nearly 1490 m (4890 ft), Cruz de Tejeda is regarded as the centre of the island. It is something of a crossroads, where traders used to set up stalls to catch the passing trade.

A stone cross stands in front of the main building, the Parador Nacional de Tejeda. From here you can see a view of the island's most famous landmark, the Roque Nublo (see page 63). The Parque Rural del Nublo at Tejeda, as the area is known, has been designated as a protected biospheric area by UNESCO.

On the way to Tejeda, watch out for further views of the rocky landmarks of the Roque Nublo, El Fraile and the Roque Bentayga. Winding roads are a feature of mountain driving on Gran Canaria and there are several on this section.

From Tejeda, head towards San Bartolomé de Tirajana and then back to Playa del Inglés along the beautiful Fataga Valley (see page 64). Watch out for an excellent viewpoint once through Fataga and out of the valley.

The Aborigen trail

The Aborigens were the pre-Hispanic inhabitants of the Canary Islands, the people who lived here before the Spaniards started to colonize the islands early in the 15th century. They are also known as the Guanches (pronounced 'wanches'), particularly so on Tenerife, but the term Aborigens is mostly favoured on Gran Canaria.

The remains and artefacts of the Aborigen culture are richer on this island than on any other in the Canaries. The original people of Gran Canaria lived with little or no interference until the Spaniards arrived. While the rest of Europe developed advanced skills in building, engineering and science, the Aborigens lived a primitive life, had no navigational skills and had not discovered metal. They lived largely in caves – the island's geology led to an abundance of such shelters – but they had the skills to build houses from stone. Exhibits at Roque Bentayga show how this ridge was inhabited by the Aborigens (see page 61).

There are strong connections in language and habits between the Aborigens and the ancient Berbers of north Africa. It is therefore possible that they may have arrived from Africa as migrants or invaders, probably around the 1st or 2nd century BC. Two kingdoms existed on the island, centred around Telde and Galdar. A hierarchical system existed within Aborigen society, with a class of nobles supporting the king. Peasants made up the largest class and they were in charge of farming, manufacturing and herding. Haircuts, beards and dress were often used as symbols to denote class.

THINGS TO SEE & DO
Arteara Necropolis ★★
Adjacent to Arteara is a genuine Aborigen necropolis, or cemetery, which has only recently been afforded the recognition and protection it deserves. To reach it, walk through the village to the far side, where there

◀ *Early life on Gran Canaria reconstructed at Mundo Aborigen*

is a sign announcing the necropolis. Take the small path to the left of the sign, which leads very shortly to the gate of the fenced enclosure. Enter through the unlocked gate and follow the path. Look uphill to the right to pick out the stone-built burial tombs. They blend in so well that they are initially difficult to see, but there are a good number around.

ⓐ On the no. 18 bus route between Playa del Inglés and Fataga
ⓒ Open daily ⓘ Admission free

Cenobio de Valerón (Convent of Valerón) ★★

Located in the north of the island, near Galdar, this honeycomb of caves in the rock face is part of Guanche history. The site is beset with tales and intrigue. The romantic will be happy to believe that this is where the 15-year-old daughters of Guanche nobility were prepared for marriage. It was believed that women with wide hips and full breasts delivered healthy children, so the girls were fed well. Others believe these caves were nothing more than a grain store. Steps lead up to the site where the keeper has trained the local lizards to feed from his hand.

🔽 *Mundo Aborigen*

Cueva Pintada (Painted Cave) ★★

Signposted from Galdar, the Cueva Pintada contains the only remaining wall paintings in the Canaries. These paintings are also reproduced in the Museo Canario (see page 17).

Forteleza de Ansite (Ansite Fort) ★

Located near Santa Lucia, the Forteleza (see page 66) is not actually a fortress, as the name suggests, but an outcrop of rock resembling a fortress. This was the final battleground in the Spanish campaign to conquer the island in 1483, where resistance by the Aborigens finally crumbled. A memorial celebration takes place here every year on 29 April.

Mundo Aborigen (Aborigens' World) ★★★

Occupying a fairly large site, Mundo Aborigen, which has been declared a place of cultural, social and historical interest by the Canarian government, is a full-scale village built to illustrate the lifestyle of the Aborigens. Wax models and tableaux are used to show the activities of these people through all stages of life, from birth to death.

The islanders believed in a supreme god, and in demons as man's enemy. Mountain tops and high areas were used as places of worship and for making sacrifices.

A touch of reality is introduced by the use of real animals in the farming area. Goats, sheep and pigs formed the mainstay of the economy. Agriculture was restricted to crops, such as barley, wheat and beans, that could survive without irrigation. Special caves were made for grain storage (see Cenobio de Valerón, opposite).

The wheel remained unknown, and the tools and pottery shown here were all made by hand. Stone, wood and bone were the basic raw materials used in almost everything manufactured. Aborigen art consisted of simple geometric designs used to decorate pottery, and cave drawings. ❷ On the no. 18 bus route between Playa del Inglés and Fataga ❶ 928 17 22 95 ❶ Open 09.00–18.00 ❶ Admission €12 ❶ Restaurant facilities available.

Mountains of the interior

Choose a clear day for this day-long 168 km (104 mile) tour (see map on page 52), which makes a circuit of all the island's high places. The highest village on the island and the highest peak are both included. Craggy mountain tops, famous rock monuments, and forests of Canarian pine all present enduring images that contrast sharply with those left behind on the coast. On a fine day, there are views of Tenerife and Mount Teide from many points on the tour.

THE ROUTE

The route starts and finishes in Playa del Inglés. Start off heading north along the Fataga valley (see page 64) to San Bartolomé de Tirajana. From here, take the road to Tejeda and prepare for a winding route. The scenery changes dramatically on passing through a cutting known as Cruz Grande. Views previously restricted to the southern section of the island open up to encompass the central mountains.

Tiny Ayacata offers a chance for a break and refreshments at the El Montañón café. Stay on the road towards Tejeda but turn left, following the signs to Roque Bentayga, when the junction is reached. The information centre lies beneath the parking area.

Roque Bentayga Interpretation Centre ★★

Roque Bentayga is more than a significant landmark gracing the skyline: it has historical significance as a pre-Hispanic religious centre and is part of an archaeological park. Exhibits show how the entire ridge was inhabited by the Aborigens (see page 57) and that many of their cave dwellings are still in existence. The sacred nature of the rock is explained and some of the cave drawings exhibited. An information leaflet in English is available. ☎ 928 66 61 89 (Tejeda tourist office)
🕐 Open 11.00–17.00

◀ *Roque Bentayga*

Return from the information centre back to the road and continue on to Tejeda, with its white cave houses clustered on a ridge. Turn left immediately after the village for Artenara. Take time along this cornice road, not just for the sweeping scenery but because of the rough road surface.

More cave houses announce the approach of Artenara, which enjoys unequalled views from its perch on the mountain side.

Artenara ★ ★ ★

At 1219 m (4000 ft), Artenara is Gran Canaria's highest village. Well situated amongst fine scenery, it is another area of cave dwellings. There is a spacious viewpoint on the edge of town with seating for picnics.

Continue through Artenara on the road towards Teror, but prepare in time for the right turn towards Cruz de Tejeda. This junction coincides with a *mirador* (viewpoint) on the left, offering expansive views of Las Palmas. Cruz de Tejeda (see page 55) provides another opportunity to stretch the legs and perhaps shop for some local produce, such as *bienmasabe*, a honey and almond sauce, or cactus jam.

Leave Cruz de Tejeda by taking the small road signposted to Los Pechos. Watch out for the Degollada de Becerra information centre, which is well worth a stop.

🔽 *Artenara*

The Lookout Interpretation Centre, Degollada de Becerra ★ ★ ★
This centre, devoted to the geology, geomorphology, wildlife and
traditions of the Nublo area, has a spectacular panoramic observation
window with a chart designed to help visitors to identify the Roque
Nublo and the surrounding rock formations. ◕ Open 11.00–17.00

Continue ahead along this road, passing over the crossroads to follow
the signs for Pozo de Nieves. The road winds around the military
establishment to end at the highest point on the island 1949 m (6394 ft).
Enjoy the unrivalled views before returning to the crossroads and
turning left. Look out very shortly for the stopping place on the right for
Roque Nublo (see below for a suggested walk). From here, the road leads
to Ayacata, where a left turn leads back to Playa del Inglés.

Roque Nublo walk ★ ★ ★
This walk takes about 1 hour and 30 minutes to complete, and sensible
footwear is essential. Start out from the car park, following the well-
defined path. It quickly starts to climb beneath the slender El Fraile, to
emerge on a saddle. Turn right here to continue climbing on to the table
area (note your access point for the return), from where Roque Nublo is
clear and obvious. Head towards the rock but prepare to return just
before reaching the base of this natural monument, when it becomes
more rocky and difficult underfoot. Return by the same route and, if you
missed El Fraile on the way up, it is more clearly visible on the way back.

> **A BITE TO EAT**
> Several small bars and restaurants in Artenara specialize in
> Canarian food, but it is advisable to check prices before ordering.
> **Mesón la Silla** A moderately priced, popular cave restaurant
> (which tends to attract coach parties). ◕ Closed Mon
> **Bar Diaz** A local spot, this bar-café is good for a snack, drink or
> quick meal. ⓐ On the main road ◕ Closed Thurs

The Fataga Valley
and the Barranco de Guayadeque

Natural curiosities and landscapes feature strongly on this 120 km (75 mile) day-long tour, and there are plenty of opportunities for stretching your legs along the route. It starts by exploring the spectacular scenery of Fataga Valley before heading back down towards sea level via Santa Lucia and on to Barranco de Guayadeque to look at the fascinating caves and cave restaurants.

THE ROUTE

This somewhat-circular tour starts and finishes in Playa del Inglés (see map, page 52). Leave Playa del Inglés by heading due north towards San Bartolomé de Tirajana. The well-surfaced but narrow road leads in a steady ascent through a barren landscape. Static figures crouched in and around buildings of natural stone mark the site of **Mundo Aborigen** (see page 59). Shortly afterwards, where the road reaches a high point, there is a good viewpoint. Parking is on the left, but on a difficult corner that requires extreme care. Having reached the upper rim of the Fataga Valley, the route now descends into it.

The Fataga Valley ★★★

The dramatic scenery of the Fataga Valley is one of the highlights of this tour. Rugged, towering mountains, set in a stark and barren countryside, decorated by nothing more than the cactus-like candlesticks of *Euphorbia canariensis*, give way to a green oasis as you progress up the valley. Nearby, palm-swamped Arteara is the location of an ancient **Aborigen necropolis** (see page 57) and **Manolo's Camel Safari** (see page 74). Higher up the valley is another green oasis, this time at Fataga, where you can stop for a coffee or refreshments. Another area of green just beyond Fataga is the site of an old mill, now the attractive location of the restaurant, the **Molina de Agua de Fataga** (see page 66).

🔺 *Fataga Valley*

On reaching San Bartolomé de Tirajana, take the road to Santa Lucia. Stop in the village for the Museo de Castello de la Forteleza, the fort-like building on the main street.

Museo de Castello de la Forteleza ★★

Natural sciences, archaeology, old weapons, folk and Aborigen artefacts rub shoulders in the 16 rooms of this well-presented museum. The castle-like building takes its name from the nearby Forteleza de Ansite (see page 66), but has no connection. The first exhibit is an old Canarian bedroom with a bed so high that steps are needed to climb in. Each room provides new surprises – stuffed birds, cases of mounted dragonflies, seashells imaginatively displayed in an old boat and even Roman *amphorae* (wine-storage jars). A restaurant and coffee bar is located in the rear gardens.

A BITE TO EAT

Molina de Agua de Fataga Originally a water mill, this is now a rural hotel and restaurant serving full meals and snacks in pleasant rural surroundings. The reasonably priced menu offers grilled sirloin, pork chops and Canarian specialities such as the stewpot with chickpeas. Take a swimming costume for a pre-lunch swim in the hotel pool. ⓐ Just beyond Fataga ① 928 17 23 03

Restaurant Tagoror Dine at moderate prices inside the cave or outside on the terrace. There is a choice of international fare and Canarian specialities. ⓐ Barranco de Guayadeque

Soon after leaving the village, stay right for Agüimes (pronounced 'Awheemehz') and look for the two huge volcanic outcrops forming the Forteleza de Ansite.

Forteleza de Ansite (Ansite Fort) ★★
Although this looks like a man-made fortress, it is an entirely natural volcanic rock. There is a viewpoint that gives an overview of the rock's history and its special significance to the Aborigens (see page 59).

From Agüimes, turn towards Ingenio but look immediately for the narrow street named 'La Orilla' on the left, just as the houses come to an end. It is badly signposted and easily missed. This takes you right into Barranco de Guayadeque.

Barranco de Guayadeque (Guayadeque Valley) ★★★
This ravine had strong connections with the Aborigens and has been declared a natural reserve. Many of the caves punctuating the walls of the ravine are still used as houses. Part-way up the valley, there is a whole cluster of cave houses which virtually constitute a village. Some of these, including a church, a bar and a restaurant, are at road level, whilst

🔺 *Santa Lucia, in the Fataga Valley*

a steep path leads up to villagers' houses buried in the rock face. Near the end of the valley is a well-organized picnic site with tables. At the head of the valley lies the **Restaurant Tagoror** (see box, opposite), worth a visit if only for a drink before you return to Playa del Inglés. For more information, contact the Agüimes Town Council office. 📞 928 12 41 83

Zoos, gardens & the Wild West

Many of the island's most popular family attractions feature animals in some way or other. From hungry crocodiles to performing parrots, there is plenty of variety on offer and amusement for all. The top attraction is Palmitos Park, but all the parks listed offer something unique.

Palmitos Park ★★★

Allow plenty of time to visit this subtropical oasis, home to some 1500 tropical birds, representing 230 species. Not all are in cages; some are in their natural setting around lakes and many are free flying. Birds apart, there is an orchid house full of exotic blooms and a huge aquarium, stocked with over 4000 brilliantly coloured saltwater fish. The tropical butterfly house, claimed to be the first in Spain, presents a natural environment where butterflies can fly freely, although they spend a lot of time at rest, when they are much harder to spot. There is also an alligator section, a walk-in bird aviary and flamingo park, and a play area for the children.

From the entrance, a one-way route leads visitors around in a systematic manner, making sure that each particular attraction is seen, although it may be necessary to back-track to the parrot show, which takes place every hour starting at 11.00 hours. Some 15 parrots spend 25 minutes amusing and entertaining the audience with a whole range of skills and tricks.

There is a pizzeria and a café on site, offering reasonably priced meals, drinks and snacks. Final call before leaving is the souvenir shop, where goods on sale have a distinct parrot flavour. After leaving the shop, keep an eye out for one more exhibit – the hard-to-spot humming birds.

Apart from all the attractions, the park is attractively laid out, with many different species of plants – all recently recatalogued – on view in the gardens. ❸ Palmitos Park, Apartado 107, Maspalomas; bus no.45 runs a frequent service from Playa del Inglés and Maspalomas, with

🔺 *Cacti at Palmitos Park*

occasional no.70 buses from Puerto Rico and the Faro
🕐 928 14 03 66/02 76 🕐 928 14 11 58 Ⓦ www.palmitospark.es
🕐 Open 10.00–18.00

Jardin Botánico Canario (Canarian Botanic Garden) ★ ★ ★
These extensive botanical gardens are devoted to the conservation
and study of the Canarian flora. Not all the gardens are on the level
– a large section ascends a steep embankment. There is a good
information centre and a restaurant. Spring is the best time to visit,
when the gardens show most colour. ⓐ Carretera de Almatriche
🕐 Open 09.00–18.00, except 1 January and Good Friday
ⓘ Admission free

Parque de Cocodrilo (Crocodile Park) ★★

Although the park boasts over 300 crocodiles, there is a much wider selection of birds and animals on show. Learn the difference between crocodiles and alligators while wandering around the various enclosed pools. There is also a snake house, an aquarium and a reptile house to visit, and a parrot show to enjoy before reaching the animal section. Lively monkeys keep children entertained while the Siberian tigers pace relentlessly. Like Palmitos Park, the grounds are well planted with exotic plants, and the cactus garden is a bold feature. ⓐ Los Corralilos ① 928 78 47 25 ⓦ www.cocodrilopark.vrcanaries.com ⓛ Open Sun–Fri 10.00–17.00, closed Sat

Banana Park ★★★

This is a new, yet typical Canarian Park on the island. The gardens offer exotic fruits, plants and flowers. There is a separate section with rescued donkeys, camels and goats. There is also an aviary with free-flying canaries and a cafeteria that provides fresh juices, snacks and beverages. Slow down the pace in the shade of an avocado tree. ⓐ Between Palmitos Park and Aqualand; bus no.45 or no.70 to Palmitos Park ① 928 14 14 75 ⓛ Open 09.30–17.00 ⓘ Adults €7, children free

Sioux City ★★★

Built originally for the stage set of an American western film back in the early 1970s, Sioux City has been preserved and developed as a Wild West theme park.

Its dusty streets can be walked without fear and trepidation for most of the day, as you case the bank or check over the Sheriff's Office, but be sure to find a shadowy corner and keep your head down at 13.30 and 16.30 hours. This is when the show springs into life and the bullets really start to fly – not to mention the cows that stampede down the main street. Evocative country-and-western music, with shades of Clint Eastwood, adds atmosphere. It is all great fun for the children and, for a few dollars more, they too can be rigged out with hats and guns.

◆ *The dusty streets of Sioux City*

Apart from the street entertainment, there is Miniature World for the children, and cowboy shows in the saloon at high noon and 15.00 hours.

Special barbecue evenings are laid on for Friday evenings throughout the year. A free drink is included with the barbecue meal and country dancing supplements the Wild West show. Ask the tourist office for further information about this. ⓐ Cañon del Aguila; bus no.29 bus to Sioux City leaves from Faro through Playa del Inglés from 09.30 hours ⓘ 928 76 25 73 ⓒ Open Tues–Sun 10.00–17.00 (Fri from 20.00 for BBQ night)

Water parks, camel safaris & go-karting

Theme parks are certainly a major form of holiday entertainment on Gran Canaria. Some of these demand active participation, and they include several aquatic parks, designed for fun in the water, as well as fairgrounds, camel safari parks and go-karting tracks where skilled experts can reach speeds of up to 80 km/h (50 mph). Here is a guide to the island's biggest and best.

● There's lots of fun to be had at water parks

Aqualand ★ ★ ★

This is the largest water park in the Canaries, featuring 29 different slides for thrill-seekers. The big slide is a straight race, with a whistle to start, but there are all sorts of slides, chutes, corkscrews and rides on a rubber ring. Announcements are made in advance when the wave machine comes into operation. A day spent here is fun for the whole family, with a small adventure playground (that carries an extra charge) for children. Sunbeds and shades are available, as well as drinks, snacks and meals, and all slides are marshalled, with lifeguards on duty.

🚌 Easily reached by Palmitos Park bus no. 45 from Playa del Inglés or Maspalomas, and bus no. 70 from Puerto Rico. Carretera Los Palmitos Park. 📞 928 14 05 25 📠 928 14 02 77 🌐 www.aqualand.es 🕐 Open daily from 10.00 ℹ Ask the tourist office about discounted tickets

Aquapark ★ ★ ★

Enough slides and chutes to keep families happy for hours, but smaller than Aqualand. Not too conveniently located, at the very rear of the town. 🚌 Motor Grande, Puerto Rico 📞 928 56 04 71 🕐 Open from 10.00 ℹ Ask the tourist office about discounted tickets

Ocean Park ★ ★

This is another aquatic park with similar features to Aqualand, but with fewer attractions. It has more water facilities for children not old enough to tackle the full-scale slides and chutes. Again, sun loungers and umbrellas are available, and refreshments. 🚌 Conveniently located in Maspalomas – easily reached from within Maspalomas and Playa del Inglés by bus nos. 30, 32 and 45. 📞 928 76 43 61 🕐 Open Mon–Fri 10.00–19.00, Sat–Sun 10.00–20.00 (summer); daily 10.00–17.00 (winter) ℹ Adults €14.50, children €10.50

Camel Safaries ★ ★ ★

It is impossible to leave Gran Canaria without riding on a camel. Trekking across the famous Maspalomas sand dunes on the back of a camel is one option (see page 39) but there are plenty of other opportunities.

It's not unusual to find a few camels waiting outside any of the major attractions, but the properly organized events provide the best experience; ask the tourist office for details.

Manolo's Camel Safari ★★★

Located in the village of Arteara in the Fataga valley, the scenic surroundings provide an ideal setting for a camel trek. Guests are welcomed with an aperitif before setting out through a palm oasis and along the valley to enjoy a simple meal out in the countryside. 🚌 The no. 18 bus passes by, but it is easiest to book through the tourist office 📞 928 79 86 80/98 📠 928 79 86 99

La Baranda Camel Safari Park ★★

Just a little further north than Manolo's, there is a straightforward camel ride on offer here, with a restaurant on site. 🚌 The no. 18 bus passes the door 📞 928 79 86 80/17 24 65 🕐 Open 09.00–18.00 ❶ Excursions: 20 min, €12; 30 min, €15; children under 10 pay half price; a small charge is made to see the camels, watch the riders or use the facilities

El Salobre Riding School & Riding Excursions ★★★

Riding lessons for beginners, treks for the more advanced. 📍 Off the Palmitos Park Road towards Tablero 📞 616 41 83 63 🌐 www.hipicachs@eresmas.com

Finca Hipisur Excursions ★★

A new centre providing excursions of two to three hours around the southern countryside. For both beginners and experienced riders. Pick up to and from your hotel, with drinks included in the price. 📞 670 64 58 57/636 47 39 70 (mobile) 📠 928 14 31 46

Gran Karting Club ★★★

Claiming the biggest track in the world – over 1600 m (1 mile) long – this is a chance to test yourself at speeds reaching 80 km/h (50 mph). There is also a junior track, suitable for children from 12–16 years, and

 Camel safaris are popular on Gran Canaria

mini-motors are available for children under 5. Clubhouse facilities include drinks and snacks. Remember to check whether your insurance is valid for this sport. There is free transport provided if the group is large.
ⓐ Tarajalillo ☎ 928 15 71 90 ☎ 639 32 97 18 (for organized competitions)
ⓕ 928 29 36 71 🕐 Open 11.00–22.00 (Apr–Sept); 10.00–21.00 (Oct–Mar)

Check at your hotel or ask your rep for discount vouchers for many of the island's attractions.

North-western Gran Canaria

The north-western corner of the island is a perfect place to escape the commotion of the principal coastal resorts, and a chance to take in some of the fascinating culture of Gran Canaria. A new road links Las Palmas with Santa María de Guía (usually called simply Guía) and Galdar, and this short tour, although an out-and-back route, is full of interest and opportunities to relax in a less-crowded part of the island.

THE ROUTE

If you are heading up towards Las Palmas (see map on page 52), take the GC3, which branches off at Jinamer/Marzagan and follow the signs to Galdar, and then to Agaete/Guia. The new 'motorway' to Agaete is well signposted, and this soon speeds you out along the northern coast of the island, with some attractive views of shingly beaches, where fishermen still cast their lines in Gran Canaria's time-honoured shore-fishing manner, next to rocky cliffs and crashing waves.

Cenobio de Valerón (Convent of Valerón) ★★

As you approach Guía, you have the opportunity to visit the Cenobio de Valerón, an amazing network of 200 caves, and one of the island's most important archaeological sites. There is a tradition that this complex of caves was the abode of Guanche priestesses, who served the God Alcorac. Another story says that it was used to prepare young noblewomen for marriage, mainly by feeding them a high-calorie diet in readiness for motherhood. A more prosaic view, however, is that the caves were used as grain warehouses, and date from the Stone Age.
🕐 Open Mon–Sat 10.00–13.00 and 15.00–17.00 ⓘ Admission free

The road soon reaches Santa María de Guía; in fact the new road bypasses the town, so you'll need to branch off. You can usually find somewhere to park along the main street.

◀ *Cenobio's honeycomb caves*

Guía ★★

The old quarter of this ancient town is quite fascinating, a maze of narrow streets, many of them cobbled, that all lead (from a pronounced bend in the main road) up to the church.

The foundation of the town took place after the conquest of the island (1483), when Pedro de Vera distributed the lands between his soldiers and native noblemen. Among the first was Sancho de Vargas Machuca, who founded the hermitage, dedicated to 'Our Lady of Guía', around which the population grew. The church itself is a beautiful piece of neo-classical work dating from the 18th century. The facade was built by locally born Luján Pérez, and it was on the organ in the church that the French composer Camille Saint-Saëns gave the first performance of some of his works during a period when he stayed and worked in Guía.

Anyone feeling in need of a little refreshment here will find the **Bar-Restaurant Tiscamanita**, on the main street, ideal, as is **Santiago Giol**, on Calle Marqués de Muni 34, where you can buy *queso de flor de Guía*, a creamy cheese, flavoured with artichoke. If you want one of the elaborately carved knives for which the island is famous, you can get one at **Rafael Torres** on Calle 18 de Julio 48, but do remember not to carry it home as hand luggage.

By continuing down the main street, you soon reach a new roundabout at the junction with the continuing motorway. Cross the roundabout and drive up towards Galdar; you'll find room to park just before the first shops and bar-restaurants on the right as you enter the town.

Galdar ★★

This is the most historic of all Aborigen towns, and very proud to be so. It is shielded from the sea by the symmetrical cone of La Montana de Galdar, and enjoys a pleasant climate. The town has an excellent covered market in the main street that is fascinating to wander around, but the *pièce de résistance* is the splendid Plaza de Santiago, a superb oasis of calm. One side of the square is occupied by the neo-classical church, which stands on the site of the palace of the former Aborigen kings.

On another corner you'll find the town hall, a magnificent building that contains in its courtyard the oldest dragon tree on the island (planted in 1718); the island's aboriginal people made use of its medicinal properties. The newly opened tourism office, stands close by the monument to Tenesor Semidan, the last king of Galdar.

Beyond Galdar, the route continues easily to Agaete, winding pleasantly across the north-western corner of the island to this prosperous little town, visited by only a small number of tourists.

Agaete ★ ★ ★

This small town stands at the mouth of the verdant Agaete *barranco*, a gathering of attractive old buildings spreading out from the main square, one of the most agreeable spots on the whole island, and well worth the journey this far to experience. But beware, it is often very difficult to find a parking space, even early in the morning.

The church here, the Iglesia de la Concepcion, has a fine 16th-century Flemish triptych that is displayed during the Bajada de la Rama, an ancient festivity celebrated both here and in the nearby harbour of Puerto de las Nieves (see Festivals & Events, page 104).

A BITE TO EAT

Agaete is the ideal place to have lunch on this tour.

Casa Nando A popular restaurant that serves really good tapas and goat's cheese. ⓐ In the old town, Calle Concepción 11

Casa Pepe Cheap, cheerful and good value. ⓐ Calle Alcalde Armas Galván 5 ⓘ 928 89 82 27 ⓒ Closed Wed

Casa Romántica International and Spanish cuisine is available at a delightful eatery that makes a point of using fresh produce. ⓓ Calle de Agaete ⓘ 928 89 80 84

Los Papayeros Savour Canarian country cooking at its best here. ⓐ Alcalde Armas Galván 22 ⓘ 928 89 80 46

Northern Gran Canaria

Despite the sudden growth in popularity of the southern part of the island, the verdant and more fertile north remains the place to experience the best of traditional Canarian culture and society. Both of the island's pre-Hispanic kingdoms had their centres here, and Las Palmas became one of the leading cities of the Spanish nation.

Inland from Las Palmas, the landscape is stunning, a rolling spread of volcanic mountains and villages where local architecture can still be found in abundance. It is all so much quieter and easy-going here; suddenly you find yourself back in time, where everything is taken at a more relaxed pace. Throughout this tour there are numerous places where you can stop off for a drink or something to eat; every village has its bar-restaurants, so choosing somewhere to take a break is easy.

THE ROUTE

From the south, take the GC1 north until the new GC3 branches off to the left to Tafira. Follow the Tafira signs until the GC3 finishes and changes into the C811, going from Tafira Baja to Tafira Alta. From Las Palmas, take the GC3 from Tamaraceite to where it joins the C811 to Tafira Baja. Between the two villages, look out for the signposted turning to the Jardín Botánico Canario. This may well be a convenient time to include it in your holiday (see page 69).

Santa Brígida ★ ★ ★

The route now winds onwards and upwards to the prosperous villa town of Santa Brígida, which has become a well-to-do suburb of Las Palmas, possessing rather less of the true Spanish atmosphere than you might expect on first impressions. Its tree-lined streets and villages with large gardens actually owe their origins to the early British settlers, who came here to begin wine-making and, later, banana-producing businesses.

◀ *The mountain village of Tejeda*

Vega de San Mateo ★★★

From Santa Brígida, the route continues to prosperous Vega de San Mateo, also known by its shortened name of San Mateo. The town stands among the foothills of the Tejeda crater. Cultivation terraces here produce substantial crops of fruit and vegetables, including almonds, chestnuts and figs. There is a popular weekend morning market here, so be warned that it becomes busy. However, if you want to take time out to wander round the market, it offers a good selection of fresh fruit and vegetables, home-grown herbs and local cheeses and wines. Perhaps not surprisingly, the town church is dedicated to the patron saint of farmers and cattle breeders.

Beyond San Mateo you head up into the Tejeda National Park, through a landscape so stunning that it is difficult not to keep stopping to admire and photograph your surroundings. Stay on the main road, ignoring diversions, and eventually you arrive at the Cruz de Tejeda, which marks the notional centre of the island, at nearly 1490 m (5000 ft) (see page 55). The square in which it is set has seen better days, but it is certainly worth trying the lunchtime restaurant here, for the exceptional terrace views, which embrace Roque Nublo and Bentayga.

A BITE TO EAT

Santa Brígida is renowned for its restaurants:

Les Grutes de Artiles A classy (and expensive) choice.

❷ Las Meleguines ☎ 928 64 05 75

Cafetería Churrería Mall Ideal for a late (or second) breakfast.

❷ Near the post office

Casa Martel This old-fashioned restaurant has an excellent wine cellar. ☎ 928 64 12 83 🕐 Open noon–17.00

Los Gerianos An inexpensive place serving grilled and roast pork and local red wine.

Tejeda ★★

For many visitors, the Cruz de Tejeda marks the turning-back point in their visit. However, this optional extension zigzags downwards into a peaceful landscape ignored by most and dotted with isolated groups of white houses with pantiled roofs. The objective of this route (which will see you later return to the Cruz) is to visit the peaceful and very attractive mountain village of Tejeda. A serpentine road descends from the Cruz to this village, which each year celebrates the Festival of the Almond Blossom, *Almendra en Flor*. Here, you can get refreshments at any of a number of small bar-restaurants – at the **Cueve da la Tea**, the **Terraza Gayfa** and the **Timagada**, for example. It is very tempting to stay in this peaceful spot for quite a while, which is a remarkable contrast if your base is somewhere like Playa del Inglés or Puerto Rico.

Go back up to Cruz, and down the road on the other side, but keep an eye open for the turning to Valleseco. On the way, and in Valleseco itself, opportunities present themselves to stop and take pictures, especially at the **Mirador de Zamora**, where the large restaurant does a lively trade.

⬤ *The mountainous north of the island*

Firgas ★ ★

Beyond this restaurant, you continue to Firgas, the 'capital' of the smallest municipality in Gran Canaria, and famed throughout the islands for its natural spring water, although it also produces bananas, watercress and yams. The main road bypasses Firgas, so if you want to spend a little time there, you will have to divert; the signposting is obvious.

Arucas ★ ★ ★

After that, head for the town of Arucas. Its most remarkable feature is the sharply pointed, neo-Gothic church of San Juan Bautista, so magnificently built it resembles a cathedral. Started in 1909, it was not completed until 1977, although it looks considerably older.

Arucas used to be known as 'the town of flowers', and it has fine subtropical gardens in the main park. Outside the town, virtually all the greenery is composed of banana plantations. North-east of the town, rises the volcanic cone of Montana de Arucas, where the last renowned aboriginal freedom fighter, Doramas, was killed in 1481. A brief visit will reward you with fine views of La Isleta and the bay of Las Palmas.

After leaving Arucas, you gradually work your way towards Las Palmas, via Tamaraceite. The way through is adequately signposted, and generally easy enough to follow.

Demand for fish, even on an island, is usually greater than the supply, so be sure to look for places that make a point of telling you they use fresh fish. You'll find tuna, cod, hake, mackerel and sardines on almost all the menus, but it's also worth trying some of the local varieties, like: red mullet; *cherne*, a kind of sea bass; *sama*, which is like sea bream; and *vieja*, a Canarian speciality, rather like parrotfish.

Food & drink

Eating out in Gran Canaria can be relatively cheap, especially in typical Canarian restaurants, although these tend to be thin on the ground in more popular tourist areas such as Playa del Inglés, where international menus predominate. For a real Canarian experience it is much better to find a restaurant frequented by the locals or head out to inland villages. Local food is delicious and certainly not to be avoided. Many traditional dishes originate from earlier times when there was a limited variety of ingredients. Later inhabitants introduced new ideas and a wider range of fruit and vegetables, to develop what has become a very wholesome and delicious cuisine.

EATING OUT

The local papers have advertisements and lists of restaurants, while in the streets, hand-outs touting for custom will give you an idea of what to expect.

⬤ A typical tapas meal

Another source of information for finding the best places to eat is the holiday company representative at your hotel; he or she will have first-hand reports from other clients. Whatever your tastes, Gran Canaria can provide for them. There is traditional British – be it full English breakfast, Sunday roast with Yorkshire puddings, bangers and mash, or fish and chips. There is even Kentucky Fried Chicken, Pizza Hut and McDonald's, if you must.

European and Asian restaurants abound, top of the list being Spanish, followed by Chinese, Indian, Italian, German, French, Scandinavian, Thai, Korean and Mexican. Popular with the Canarians are Venezuelan restaurants – try their freshly prepared *arepas*, savoury South American pancakes.

Every Canarian town and village has a bar or two and practically all will be able to produce food, so one never needs to go hungry.

LOCAL FOOD

Once a staple food of the pre-Hispanic population, *gofio*, toasted maize or wheat, ground into flour, is still a feature in many recipes. It was once made into bread, but is now used as a thickener or made into dumplings. Canarian soups are more like stews and are virtually a meal

TAPAS

An interesting way to sample a variety of Canarian dishes is to seek out a tapas bar – the Spaniards' own version of a fast-food outlet. There are many such bars in Las Palmas and in local communities, but you will be hard pressed to find one in tourist areas. Tapas are served in small portions (*tapa* means 'lid' or small dish) but if something more substantial is required, ask for a medium size – *medio ración* – or a large portion to share between two – a *ración* (pronounced 'rasslon'). The problem here is knowing what to ask for, so go armed with the names of some dishes or be brave and choose at random from the display on the counter.

Treat yourself to a traditional meal

in themselves, so choose carefully if you are aiming for three courses. Fresh vegetables are plentiful, as is fish (salted and fresh), which is usually boiled, fried or grilled and served with a *mojo* (pronounced 'mocko') sauce. Meats, such as goat, rabbit and pork, are found locally, but other meat – steak for example – is imported especially for tourists. Cheese, mostly made from goat's milk, is an important accompaniment to a meal, and the Canaries boast many varieties – mild *queso flor*, 'flower cheese', from Guí, is a popular choice.

WINE

A small quantity of wine is still produced near Las Palmas, but the large selection of wine in the shops is imported from mainland Spain. Two reasonably priced Riojas are Campo Vieja and Siglo, but there is a huge selection to sample.

Gran Canaria and the other islands have cheaper prices for alcoholic drinks than mainland Spain and the rest of the EU. It is usually wise to ask specifically for a brand name, as the cheaper Spanish alternatives may not be to your liking.

There is an incredible selection of spirits, but be warned that measures are triple or quadruple the size of British measures. The *ron* (rum) is a white spirit made on Gran Canaria from sugar cane. It is consumed by the locals, who often drink it with coffee. *Ron miel*, a dark liqueur, is a mixture of rum and honey – warming on a cool evening. Or you could try the unique, sweet flavour of the banana liqueur, *cobana*. This makes an unusual souvenir as it is sold in a bottle shaped like a bunch of bananas.

International makes of canned beers are now widely available, such as Skol, Worthington and even Guinness. The local lager, Dorada, comes on tap and in cans and is quite thirst quenching. Sangria, a mixed drink served in a big glass jug with lots of fruit and ice, is often chosen by tourists. Beware – this attractive looking drink can be very alcoholic. More innocuous is *zumo*, which is made from freshly squeezed fruit juices. Try a mixture of *naranja* (orange), *limón* (lemon) and *melocotón* (peach).

Menu decoder

aceitunas en mojo Olives in hot sauce
bocadillo (bocadee-yo) Filled roll
ensalada Salad

helado Ice cream
perrito caliente Hot-dog
tapas Snacks

TYPICAL CANARIAN DISHES

cabrito Kid (goat)
caldo de escado Fish, vegetables and maize meal stew
chipirones Small squid
conejo al salmorejo Rabbit in hot chilli sauce
gambas ajillo Garlic prawns
garbanzasa Chickpea stew with meat
lomo Slices of pork
pata de cerdo Roast leg of pork
pechuga empanada Breaded chicken breast or chicken breast
   in batter
potage Thick vegetable soup – may contain added meat
potage de berros Watercress soup
puchero Meat and vegetable stew
queso Cheese
ranchos Noodles, beef and chickpeas
ropa vieja Chickpeas, vegetables and potatoes (although meat can be
   added)
sancocho Salted fish (often *cherne*, a kind of sea bass) with potatoes
   and sweet potatoes

DESSERTS

arroz con leche Cold rice pudding
bienmesabe A mix of honey and almonds (delicious poured over
   ice cream)
flan Crème caramel
fruta del tiempo Fresh fruit in season
truchas Turnovers filled with pumpkin jam

Papas arrugadas (small jacket potatoes boiled in very salty water) served with a *mojo picante* (hot chilli sauce) or *mojo verde* (herb and garlic sauce) make an ideal snack at lunchtime. Those with a light appetite might find one dish between two is sufficient.

DRINKS

agua (pronounced *ah-whah*)

mineral Mineral water
con gas/sin gas Fizzy/still

batido Milkshake
café Coffee

con leche Made with milk
cortado Small white coffee
descafeinado Decaffeinated
solo Black

cerveza Beer
leche Milk
limonada Lemonade
naranja Orange
ron Local rum
té Tea
vino Wine

blanco White
rosado Rosé
tinto Red

SPECIALITY DRINKS

bitter kas Similar to Campari but non-alcoholic
Cocktail Atlantico Rum, dry gin, banana liqueur, blue curaçao, pineapple nectar
Cocktail Canario Rum, banana cream liqueur, orange juice, cointreau, a drop of grenadine
guindilla Rum-based cherry liqueur
mora Blackberry liqueur
ron miel Rum-with honey, a local speciality
sangria Mix of red wine, spirits and fruit juices; can be made with champagne on request

Shopping

Although part of the EU, Gran Canaria has special duty-free status, so it is treated as a non-EU territory for allowances. This means that, tempting as it is to spend and spend on the duty-free goods that dominate many of the shopping centres, there is a limit to the value of goods (and separate allowance for tobacco and alcohol) that can be brought back to the UK without attracting import tax. These allowances vary, so ask for information on the latest duty-free allowances.

BARGAINING

Expect to bargain in markets and at many of the duty-free shops, and note that marked prices are usually highly inflated.

A simple technique for bargaining is to show an interest in the goods and then start to walk away. The price drops instantly, so show renewed interest, and then turn away again. Another price reduction will be offered. This is the starting point for making an offer. It is not advisable to spend serious money without first checking out a few suppliers.

🔻 *Bargain hunting at the local market*

SOUVENIRS

If you are looking for souvenirs unique to the island, you might consider:

▲ *Handmade fans*

- Baskets made from woven banana leaves or rushes, such as might be seen in Teror.
- A knife with a handle inlaid with bone and horn (take this home in a suitcase, not in hand luggage, or you risk having it confiscated as an offensive weapon).
- Lace, especially from Ingenio, Agüimes and Tirjana. Lace and linen tablecloths are also freely available in the markets. These are often imported but they can still be good value. Goods carrying a FEDAC label guarantee that the product has been made by craftspeople.
- *Bienmesabe* (a honey and almond sauce), and melon, almond and peach liqueurs.

Watches and designer-label clothes sold at give-away prices, especially from roadside stalls and street hawkers, are almost certain to be counterfeit – be sure not to pay too high a price.

AIRPORT SHOPPING

The departure lounge has an extensive shopping mall, complete with Burger King, sandwich bars, restaurants, cafés and play areas for children. Enjoy last-minute duty-free shopping for clothing – from **Tie Rack**, **Leather House** and **American World** – for Canarian specialities and souvenirs, and for flowers. Goods in the airport are no cheaper than those sold in the shops in Gran Canaria, since the whole island is a duty-free area.

Kids

There is plenty to entertain children on Gran Canaria. Mountains of sand surround the southern coastal resorts and the deep dunes at Maspalomas provide endless hours of fun. Off the beach there are enough activities to keep children happily occupied.

FUN WITH THE ANIMALS

Children are fascinated by animals and there are plenty of zoos and theme parks to visit. Palmitos Park, with 1500 exotic birds, is perhaps the biggest and best organized on the island, but both Banana Park and Parque de Cocodrilo, with more than 350 crocodiles, are equally absorbing (see pages 68–71).

Sioux City offers Wild West shows and plans to improve its attractions for children. Increasing the number of animals is at the heart of the scheme and the intention is to import 15 mini-horses, four mini-donkeys and 12 American buffalo. There will also be a Ferris wheel. Birthday parties can be arranged for children at Sioux City at fairly short notice (see page 70 for further details). Camel rides are also available at many places on the island (see page 73–74).

◗ *Spot the croc*

MINI-GOLF

Plenty of mini-golf facilities are open late, so it is not necessary to surrender prime beach time. The first of two in Playa del Inglés, **Taidia Mini-Golf**, has a pool table and drinks. ⊘ Avenida de Tirajana (Tirahana), behind Supermercado Cadena Maraga ❶ Open 10.00–00.30 ❶ Small charge. Another is **San Valentine Park** ⊘ Calle Timple ❶ 928 76 24 65 ❶ Open 09.00–23.00 ❶ Small charge

THE MINI-TREN

The Mini-Tren, or Choo-Choo train, tours the streets of Playa del Inglés. Children and families ride in open but shaded carriages in a long snake behind the engine. It must be joined at Avenida Italia 12.

SWIMMING, DIVING & GO-KARTING

There is a pleasant swimming pool behind the beach in Puerto Rico, which caters well for children, not to mention the big water parks such as Aqualand and Ocean Park (detailed on pages 73). Gran Karting Club (see page 74) has the largest go-karting track in Spain, but also caters for children. Apart from the junior track, suitable for children between the ages of 12 and 16, there are mini-motors for children under 5 to try out. Mini-bikes are a more recent addition to the entertainment, and are suitable for those over the age of 10. Or try a thrilling trip to the bottom of the sea on the *Yellow Submarine* in Puerto de Mogán (see page 43).

🔺 *Fun for all the family*

Sports & activities

Good sea temperatures throughout the year are an advantage for sea sport enthusiasts on Gran Canaria. This makes conditions for water sports ideal around the shores of the island, which hosts more than its share of international events. September is the warmest month, when sea temperatures reach an average of 23.3°C (74°F) while winter temperatures remain around 19°C (67°F), just dipping below in March. Puerto Rico is one of the island's most important centres for water activities, while golf courses, horse riding and bike tours are also on offer throughout the island.

CRUISING

Cruising is perhaps a grand term, but there are one or two boats offering sea trips with entertainment, lunch and opportunities for swimming.

Dolphin search trip

The *Spirit of the Sea*, a glass-bottomed catamaran based in Puerto Rico, offers two-hour trips to look for dolphins and whales. ❶ 928 56 22 29 ⓔ spirit@dolphin-whale.com ⓦ www.dolphin-whale.com ⓛ Trips leave daily at 10.00, 12.30 and 15.00

Supercat

Supercat I is claimed to be the world's largest catamaran and offers daytime and evening cruises that can be booked through holiday reps, hotels or directly. ❷ Puerto Rico harbour ❶ 928 15 02 48/73 56 56, or 900 50 62 60 (for free calls) ❶ 928 73 58 00

Timanfaya

Another sailing ship offering excursions. ❷ Out of Puerto Rico harbour; a special passenger bus runs from Playa del Inglés, with various pick-up points along the way ❶ 928 26 82 80/900 70 02 22

◆ *Try your hand at windsurfing*

GOLF

Anfi Tauro Golf A nine-hole golf course. @ Near Mogán by the Time Share complex ☎ 928 12 88 40/41 Ⓦ www.anfi.com

Bandama Golf Club Founded originally in Las Palmas in 1891, this golf club was relocated to Bandama in 1956. The 18-hole, par-71 course, designed by Mackenzie Ross, is a fairly testing 5679 m (6213 yards) long. Facilities include a good clubhouse and restaurant, practice tees, two putting greens and a sports shop. @ Santa Brígida, 14 km (nearly 9 miles) from Las Palmas, adjacent to the Bandama Crater ☎ 928 35 10 50 ☎ 928 35 10 50/11 04 @ rcglp@step.es ⏰ Open daily, closed Sat and holidays

Salobre Golf An 18-hole course with clubhouse, café and restaurant. @ Situated in the mountains behind Pasito Blanco off the GC1, 53 km (33 miles) south from Maspalomas ☎ 928 01 01 03/06 18 28 ☎ 928 01 01 04/828 06 18 29 Ⓦ www.salobregolfresort.com

Campo de Golf Located adjacent to the famous sand dunes in Maspalomas, this 18-hole, par-73 course is long, at 6216 m (6800 yards). Other facilities include a driving range, putting green, and trolley and club hire. Apart from a clubhouse, there is a restaurant and snack service. @ Avenida Neckerman, Maspalomas ☎ 928 76 25 81/76 73 43 ☎ 928 76 82 45 Ⓦ www.maspalomasgolf.net ⏰ Special rates are offered to juniors under the age of 18

🔽 *Campo de Golf*

Cortijo Club de Campo This new 18-hole course with lakes and palm trees is 6 km (4 miles) from Las Palmas and ten minutes' north from the airport. ⓐ Autopista del Sur GC1, Km 6.4, 35218 Telde ⓣ 928 68 48 90/69 71 50 ⓕ 928 71 49 05 ⓦ www.elcortijo.es

HORSE RIDING

Hipisur This place has a horse-riding section for beginners or veteran riders. ⓐ Based in Maspalomas (pick up from your hotel) ⓣ 928 14 31 46
Beniarab Riding School ⓣ 928 14 20 18/629 53 41 55 ⓕ 928 14 02 20
El Salobre Riding School (see page 74).

QUAD SAFARIS & BIKE TOURS

For the adventurous, there is always the possibility of going on a mountain-bike tour, or a quad bike safari, driving along dry river beds and mountain paths. For those who prefer a more leisurely pace, a good option is a bicycle tour, on paved roads to places of beauty.
Free Motion Tours ⓣ 928 77 7 4 79 ⓕ 928 77 52 99
ⓔ info@free-motion.net ⓦ www.free-motion.net

SAILING & WINDSURFING SCHOOLS

There are several schools on the island offering sailing and windsurfing tuition for all levels:
Real Club Victoria Offers windsurfing lessons for children and adults, and Optimist sailing for children 8–14. ⓐ Paseo de las Canteras 4, Las Palmas ⓣ 928 46 06 30 (club), 928 46 25 14/46 24 72 (school)

SCUBA DIVING

Classes for beginners are offered by a number of schools on the island, and there are plenty of opportunities for diving for the more experienced:
Aquanauts Dive Centre ⓐ On the beachfront at Puerto Rico
ⓣ 928 56 06 55 ⓔ info@aquanauts-divecenter.com

Calypso Divers Diving excursions for all levels. English spoken, and all equipment provided. ❷ Hotel Mirador. Mapalomas, Sonneland
❶/❻ 928 76 94 64 ⓦ www.divingcalypso.net
Centro Nautico de Buceo Equipment for 40 divers. ❷ Hotel IFA Interclub Atlantic, San Agustín ❶ 928 77 02 00 ❺ Open 09.00–18.00
Padi Diving School/Nordic Divers ❷ Based at the Aeroclub
❶ 660 29 18 91 (mobile) ⓦ www.lgdiving.com
Top Diving Provides organized group expeditions. ❷ Puerto Rico
❶ 928 56 06 09 ❺ Departures at 10.00 hours and 14.00 hours

SEA FISHING

Off-shore fishing is especially good around the island, with the opportunity to fish for tuna, shark, white and blue swordfish and shark. Some of the boats available include:
Barakuda II This boat's length is 12 m (40 ft), with a beam of 4.4 m (17 ft). Rods and materials are provided, and sandwiches and drinks are available. An English- and German-speaking skipper are each available with advice. Two days' notice required. ❶ 928 73 50 80/689 16 88 15
Sea fishing ❷ Leaving from Puerto Rico ❶/❻ 928 56 55 21, ask for Antonio; alternatively ❶ 659 69 24 25/609 56 42 94 (ask for Roberto)

SURFING

This is a year-round activity on Gran Canaria, but the best waves are generally experienced between September and March. The north, near Galdar, offers the most challenging conditions, with waves as high as 5 m (16 ft) at times. When the wind is in the east, a good place for surfing is in the Bay of Pozo Izquierdo. In the south, the beach just west of the lighthouse in Maspalomas and Arguineguin provides a good spot.

TENNIS & SQUASH

Tenis Holican ❷ Holanda, Maspalomas ❶ 928 76 77 46

WALKING

Some 308 km (186 miles) of footpaths have already been restored on the island for walkers to enjoy, and work continues to repair and re-build more of these. All paths are in the upland areas towards the centre and north of Gran Canaria. Unfortunately, information about the paths has not managed to keep up with the pace of restoration. The best walking book, available at bookshops on the island, is *Landscapes of Gran Canaria*, published by Sunflower Books, and this is revised regularly, or you can contact the Gran Canaria Tourist Board. ❶ 928 44 68 24/77 15 50 /66 61 89 Ⓦ www.maspalomas-web.org

WATERSKIING

Puerto Rico offers the best centre for practising this sport: **Martin's** offers lessons in waterskiing. ⓐ Francisco Martín Pavón, Puerto Escala, Puerto Rico ❶ 678 53 54 94 Ⓛ Open Tues–Sun 10.00–18.00, closed Mon

WINDSURFING

There are two particular places in the north of the island, near Gáldar and at Puerto de la Nieves, which are highly favoured by expert windsurfers, but generally the southern-most part of the island provides conditions more suitable for beginners and advanced levels.

Equipment can be hired at many beaches in the south, but there are two windsurfing schools that offer tuition to both beginners and improvers:

Club Mistral Canarias ⓐ S L Playa de Tarajalillo ❶ 928 15 71 58 Ⓛ Open 09.30–17.00

Puerto Rico Sailing School ⓐ Puerto Rico, Puerto Escala ❶ 928 56 52 92/609 58 59 33 Ⓛ Open Mon–Sat, closed Sun and August for holidays

Festivals & events

There is nothing the Canarians enjoy more than a good fiesta. Any significant event is celebrated and turned into a street party. Some fiestas have deep religious significance but most are a lively mixture of fun and exuberance.

Every village celebrates the feast day of its own patron saint, with local and national days to celebrate as well. **Carnaval**, the greatest and most colourful of them all, takes place in February or March, to coincide with the start of Lent. Celebrations across the island culminate in a grand fancy-dress party and a masked parade that goes on for hours.

In Playa del Inglés, Carnaval takes over the Yumbo Centre for about two weeks and there are many local events organized, including in the Parque Santa Catalina or the Plaza Santa Ana in Las Palmas. The curtain finally descends with a solemn procession for the Burial of the Sardine.

Other important celebrations include:
- The Feast of the Three Kings on 6 January; this marks the Canarian Christmas and is widely celebrated on the island.
- The Almond Blossom Festival, around late February in Tejeda.
- May Day is a holiday which is usually celebrated by parades, although they often take place on the first Sunday in May.
- Corpus Christi, 17 June, is special in Las Palmas. The streets around the cathedral are decorated with flowers, sand and pebbles made into patterns and pictures.
- Teror observes its own special day, 8 September, with the most important religious celebration on the island.

CANARY WRESTLING
This unusual sport is very popular on Gran Canaria. Traditionally, the wrestling takes place in a sand-covered arena and involves a team of 12 people. The loser is the one who touches the ground with any part of the body (apart from the feet) during a hold.

MUSIC FESTIVAL ATLANTA

Every year, during the month of March, a two-day music festival, with acts from Spain, Britain and other countries, is held on the beach in Playa del Inglés. The date varies, so check with the tourist office. It is especially popular with the under 30s.

SAN FERNANDO FAIR

This lively affair takes place for a week in May each year, with all the usual fun of the fair, plenty of side shows and entertainment for all ages.

WHAT'S ON WHEN

Gran Canaria has an amazing wealth of festivals and celebrations. There is almost certainly one taking place during your stay. For festival information: ☎ 928 77 15 50 🌐 www.grancanaria.com

January

- Feast of the Three Kings (see page, opposite).

February

- Almond Blossom Festival (see page, opposite): celebrated in Valsequillo and Tejeda. Lots of music and dancing, food and drink.
- Carnaval (see page, opposite): a week of celebrations to the music of street bands and dance groups, parades and all-night street parties.

March

- Arguineguin: Feast Day of Santa Agueda.

April

- Fiesta de los Aborigenes: commemorates the defeat of the indigenous people. Held on 29 April in Las Palmas; lots of music and dancing.

May

- Apricot Festival in Fataga.

June

- Corpus Christi (see page 102) in Las Palmas and Arucas. Carpets of flowers, sawdust and sand cover the route of a procession.

July

- Fiestas del Carmen: 16 July. Celebrated in traditional fishing villages.
- Romeria al Señor de los Caballeros: held in Galdar on 25 July. Goes on for about 20 days, with Canarian music, dancing and wrestling.

August

- Bajada de la Rama: Agaete's fiesta, 4 August. An aboriginal festival, from pre-Hispanic days – the island's most popular festival.

September

- Feast of Our Lady of the Pine: the island's patron saint, on 8 September in Teror. A great and moving pilgrimage – many walk to Teror through the night to render homage, with singing and dancing.
- Fiesta del Charco: in San Nicolás de Tolentino on 10 September A traditional immersion in water that is re-enacted each year.

October

- Fiestas de Buestra Señora del Rosario: on 5 October in Agüimes, with traditional stick fighting, Canarian wrestling and flower battles.
- La Naval: on 6 October in Las Palmas. Commemorates the successful repulsion of Sir Francis Drake from the islands in 1595.

November

- Rancho de Animas: peculiar to Teror – between November and January. Groups of mainly elderly men roam the streets singing.

December

- Fiesta de los Labradores: Santa Lucia, on 20 December. Everyone celebrates by dressing in peasant costume.
- Feast Day of Santa Lucia: 13 December.

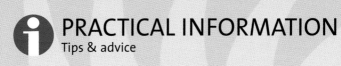

Preparing to go

GETTING THERE

The cheapest way to get to Gran Canaria is to book a package holiday with one of the leading tour operators specializing in Gran Canarian holidays. You should also check the travel supplements of the weekend newspapers, such as the *Sunday Telegraph* and the *Sunday Times*. They often carry adverts for inexpensive flights, as well as classified adverts for privately owned villas and apartments to rent in most popular holiday destinations.

If your travelling times are flexible, and if you can avoid the school holidays, you can also find some very cheap last-minute deals using the websites for the leading holiday companies.

If you would prefer the services of a small, independent specialist, try **Travellers' Way**. This company specializes in rural tourism, and has a good selection of hotel and self-catering holidays on the islands, with converted farm buildings (*casas rurales*) at reasonable prices. ❸ The Barns, Hewell Lane, Bromsgrove, Worcs B60 1LP ❶ 01527 55 90 00 ❶ 01527 83 61 59 ❿ www.secretdestinations.com

BY AIR

The Canary Islands are a four-hour flight from the UK. The majority of visitors to the islands use charter companies, which operate from nearly all of the UK's regional airports. Only the Spanish national carrier, **Iberia Airlines**, offers scheduled flights to Gran Canaria, though this usually means changing in Madrid or Barcelona. ❸ UK office: Iberia House, 10 Hammersmith Broadway, London W6 7AL ❶ 0870 49 91 305 ❶ 00 349 17 46 16 53 (24 hours – in Spain) ❿ www.iberia.com

BY SHIP

The only passenger and vehicle shipping line to operate a regular service between mainland Spain and the Canary Islands is the ferry company **Trasmediterranea**, which runs several services a week from Cadiz to Gran Canaria, Lanzarote and Tenerife.

Trasmediterranea's UK agent is **Southern Ferries**. ☎ First Floor, 179 Piccadilly, London W1V 9DB ☎ 0870 499 1305 (from Gran Canaria) ☎ 902 454 645 ☎ 0870 499 1304 ✉ nfo@thelatintraveller.com ⊕ www.trasmediterranea.es ❶ Early bookings are necessary for school holidays and at carnival time (February); tickets include all meals during the 48- to 72-hour voyage; pensioners get a 20 per cent discount

INTER-ISLAND SERVICES

A complex network of inter-island ferries and hydrofoils links the seven main islands of the Canaries, and schedules change very regularly, so you need to check times locally. To reach La Palma, La Gomera, El Hierro and Fuerteventura, it is necessary to take the inter-island ferries. Most of the inter-islands services are operated by Trasmediterranea (all passenger enquiries, see 'By Ship', opposite) or the **Fred Olsen Line**. ☎ Edificio Fred Olsen, Poligono Industrial Añaza, Santa Cruz de Tenerife ☎ 928 49 50 46/902 10 01 07 ☎ 928 49 50 31 (for timetable details and booking) ⊕ www.fredolsen.es. The local airline **Binter Canarias** provides regular flights between the islands. ☎ Aeropuerto de Gran Canaria, Parcela 9 del ZIMA, Apartado 50, 35230 Gran Canaria ☎ 928 57 96 01 ⊕ www.bintercanarias.es

BEFORE YOU LEAVE

Holidays should be about fun and relaxation, so avoid last-minute panics and stress by making your preparations well in advance.

It is not necessary to have inoculations to travel in Europe, but you should make sure you and your family are up to date with the basics, such as tetanus. It is a good idea to pack a small first-aid kit to carry with you, containing plasters, antiseptic cream, travel sickness pills, insect repellent and/or bite relief cream, antihistamine tablets, upset stomach remedies and painkillers. Sun lotion can be more expensive in Gran Canaria than in the UK, so it is worth taking a good selection, especially of the higher factor lotions if you have children with you, and don't forget after-sun cream as well. If you are taking prescription medicines, ensure that you take enough for the duration of your visit, and an extra copy of the information sheet in case of loss, but you may find it impossible to obtain the exact same medicines in Gran Canaria. It is also worth having a dental check-up before you go.

DOCUMENTS

The most important documents you will need are your tickets and your passport. Check well in advance that your passport is up to date and has least three months left to run (six months is even better). All children, including newborn babies, need their own passport, unless they are already included on the passport of the person they are travelling with. It takes at least three weeks to process a passport renewal. This can be longer in the run-up to the summer. Contact the **Passport Agency** for the latest information. ☏ 0870 521 0410 ✉ info@passport.gov.uk ⓦ www.ukpa.gov.uk

You should check the details of your travel tickets well before your departure, ensuring that the timings and dates are correct.

If you are a UK resident thinking of hiring a car while you are away, you will need to have your UK driving licence with you. If you want more than one driver for the car, the other drivers must have their licence too.

MONEY

You will need some currency before you go, especially if your flight gets you to your destination at the weekend or late in the day after the banks have closed. Traveller's cheques are the safest way to carry money because the money will be refunded if the cheques are lost or stolen. To buy traveller's cheques or exchange money at a bank, you may need to give up to a week's notice, depending on the quantity of foreign currency you require. You can exchange money at the airport before you depart. You should also make sure that your credit, charge and debit cards are up to date – you do not want them to expire mid-holiday – and that your credit limit is sufficient for holiday purchases. Don't forget, too, to check your PIN numbers in case you haven't used them for a while – you may want to draw money from cash dispensers while you are away. Ring your bank or card company and they will help you out.

INSURANCE

Do you have sufficient cover for your holiday? Check that your policy covers you adequately for loss of possessions and valuables, for activities you might want to try – such as scuba-diving, horse-riding, or water sports – and for emergency medical and dental treatment, including flights home, if required.

After January 2006, a new EHIC card replaces the E111 form to allow UK visitors access to reduced-cost, and sometimes free state-provided medical treatment in the EEA. For further information, ring EHIC enquiries line: ☎ 0845 605 0707, or visit the Department of Health website ⓦ www.dh.gov.uk

CLIMATE

Gran Canaria has so many tourists because the weather is almost guaranteed to be good. The average temperature ranges between 23 and 28°C (75 and 85°F). The island has three temperature belts. The north of the island, which includes Las Palmas southwards down to Vecindario, is the coolest band. The adjacent band runs from Vecindario South to Playa del Ingles, and the band next to this runs from Playa to the southern tip of the island, which includes Puerto Rico and Mogan. Each one of these bands has a temperature variation of 2°C (5–7°F) from the adjacent one, with the hottest band being in the south. The weather can be quite a bit cooler in the mountains, especially between the months of November to the end of May, so always take a light jacket or cardigan with you if you go during these months.

Because the island is much closer to the equator than other holiday areas, you will burn very quickly, even on a cloudy day. Always take precautions against the sun.

TELEPHONING GRAN CANARIA
To call Gran Canaria from the UK, dial 00 34 then the nine-digit number – there's no need to wait for a dialling tone.

SECURITY

Take sensible precautions to prevent your house being burgled while you are away:

- Cancel milk, newspapers and other regular deliveries so that post and milk does not pile up on the doorstep, indicating that you are away.
- Let the postman know where to leave parcels and bulky mail (ideally with a next-door neighbour) that will not go through your letterbox.
- If possible, arrange for a friend or neighbour to visit regularly, closing and opening curtains in the evening and morning, and switching lights on and off to give the impression that the house is being lived in.
- Consider buying electrical-timing devices that will switch lights and radios on and off, again to give the impression that there is someone in the house.
- Let Neighbourhood Watch representatives know that you will be away so that they can keep an eye on your home.
- If you have a burglar alarm, make sure that it is serviced and working properly and is switched on when you leave (you may find that your insurance policy requires this). Ensure that a neighbour is able to gain access to the alarm to turn it off if it is set off accidentally.
- If you are leaving cars unattended, put them in a garage, if possible, and leave a key with a neighbour in case the alarm goes off.

SPECIAL MEALS

Do not forget that you need to book special in-flight meals (for example vegetarian, vegan or diabetic) well in advance – preferably when the booking is made, but otherwise at least two weeks in advance of your departure.

AIRPORT PARKING & ACCOMMODATION

If you intend to leave your car in an airport car park while you are away, or stay the night at an airport hotel before or after your flight, you should book well ahead to take advantage of discounts or cheap off-airport parking. Airport accommodation gets booked up several weeks in advance, especially during the height of the holiday season. Check whether the hotel offers free parking for the duration of the holiday – often the savings made on parking costs can significantly reduce the accommodation price.

BAGGAGE ALLOWANCES

Baggage allowances vary according to the airline, destination and the class of travel, but 20 kg (44 lb) per person is the norm for luggage that is carried in the hold (it usually tells you what the weight limit is on your ticket). You are also allowed one item of cabin baggage weighing no more than 5 kg (11 lb), and measuring 46 by 30 by 23 cm (18 by 12 by 9 inches). In addition, you can carry your duty-free purchases, umbrella, handbag, coat, camera, etc, as hand baggage. Large items – surfboards, golf-clubs, collapsible wheelchairs and pushchairs – are usually charged as extras and it is a good idea to let the airline know in advance that you want to bring these.

CHECK-IN, PASSPORT CONTROL & CUSTOMS

First-time travellers can often find airport security intimidating, but it is all very easy, really.

- Check-in desks usually open two to three hours before the flight is due to depart. Seats are allocated on a first-come, first-served basis, so those who arrive early get the best choice of seats. Most airlines require you to book in two hours ahead of the flight, and the flight will probably close about 20 to 30 minutes before scheduled take-off time – if at all possible, try and let the airline know if you are delayed.
- On arrival at the airport, look for your flight number on the TV monitors in the check-in area, and find the relevant check-in desk. Your tickets will be checked and your luggage labelled. You will be given a boarding card indicating the gate number where you will board your plane.
- You can then proceed to the departure gate, where your boarding pass will be checked. Next you will go through a security check, during

which your hand luggage will be X-rayed (do not worry – this does not damage camera film, magnetic disks or tapes); you will then pass through a metal-detector gate, where your clothing may be searched if anything you are carrying sets off the alarm. Last of all, your passport will be checked, and that's it – you're through to the departure area.

- In the departure area, you can shop and relax, but keep an eye on the monitors that tell you when your flight is ready to board – usually about 30 minutes before take-off time. Go to the departure gate indicated on the monitor and on your boarding card and follow the instructions given to you by the airline staff.

During your stay

AIRPORTS

The airport in Gran Canaria caters very well for tourists, with a range of sandwich bars and a restaurant. There is always a cafeteria open for drinks and snacks for those who have to leave during the night. There is also a children's play area where the little ones can while away the waiting time for the flight. There is a wide selection of shops for last-minute purchases, gifts and for local crafts, ceramics and plants. These shops are open 08.00–21.00 hours. The duty-free shop opens at the same time, but closes later, depending whether there is anyone in the shop. When buying things from the airport, remember that most things are cheaper in the resort areas.

BEACHES

In summer, many beaches have life guards and a flag safety system. Other beaches may be safe for swimming but there are unlikely to be lifeguards or life-saving amenities available. Bear in mind that the strong winds in the hotter months can quickly change a safe beach into a not-so-safe one, and some can have strong currents the further out that you go. If in doubt, ask your local representative or at your hotel.

BEACH SAFETY

Most beaches where the public bathe in numbers operate a flag system to indicate the sea conditions.

- Red (or black): dangerous – no swimming
- Yellow: good swimmers only – apply caution
- Green (or white): safe bathing conditions for all

CHILDREN'S ACTIVITIES

Gran Canaria provides a variety of different entertainment for children, ranging from in-resort activities, such as kids' clubs run by the hotel/complex staff, to BBQ night at Sioux City. If there is a kids' club in your hotel/complex, check on the age limit for the children and how many children there are to each minder. Ask if it is free or if you have to pay, otherwise you might receive an unexpected big bill at the end of your stay. Make sure you take note of the opening hours – you don't want to come back to a tearful child and angry hotel staff because you arrive two hours after the club finishes.

Be careful not to go to places like Palmitos Park, Sioux City or any of the water parks if it is a really scorching hot day. There are many things to do in the evening, when the heat of the sun has gone. There is the mini-train, and most of the big shopping/restaurant complexes, like the Cita and along the Avenida de Tirajana, have a mini-golf and skittles area.

If you go to any of the animal or plant parks, remember to take plenty of drinking water with you, as you will probably be walking around for a good few hours. Always make sure that children wear some sort of protective covering on their heads – and it's not a bad idea for grown-ups to do the same! All of the water parks forbid the wearing of T-shirts when on any of the apparatus, which means that children are advised to wear their T-shirts until the last moment when queuing for a slide to avoid excessive exposure to the sun.

CONSULATE

The British Consulate in Las Palmas has British staff as well as some Spanish staff who speak excellent English. You can sometimes catch them 30 minutes (by telephone) before and after opening and closing hours. ☎ 928 26 25 08/26 58 (it may be engaged for some time) 🕐 Open Mon–Fri 09.00–14.00 except national holidays. Closed Sat and Sun

CURRENCY

Money Spain entered the single currency on 1 Jan 2002. Euro (€) note denominations are 500, 200, 100, 50, 20, 10 and 5. Coins are 1 and 2 euros and 1, 2, 5, 10, 20 and 50 céntimos. The UK is not part of the European Monetary System, so the value of the Euro against the British pound varies.

Exchange Traveller's cheques and Eurocheques can all be used to pay bills or obtain money. Banks are open Monday to Friday 08.30–14.00 (some until 16.00); Saturday 09.00–13.00. Hotel receptions, travel agents and banks will exchange your cash, but *take note* there are practically no exchange bureaux due to the Euro being the European common currency now. Wherever you elect to change money, take your passport.

Credit cards These are accepted in all resorts.

CUSTOMS

Tourism has only come to the Canaries within the last 20 to 30 years, so there are not many customs the locals expect tourists to uphold. However, it is worth trying to speak Spanish, even if you can only manage very little. There are no restrictions on entering the churches, but respectful behaviour is expected (not making a lot of noise, no smoking, eating or drinking). Don't be offended if the local people do not say 'please' or 'thank you'. It doesn't seem to be in the vocabulary!

ELECTRICITY

You will need an adaptor plug for electrical appliances, which can be bought from any major retail outlet in the UK or from most of the tourist shops on the island. The voltage is 220, slightly less than in the

UK, but it won't affect the appliance. If you are not careful when removing a plug in your hotel room, the whole electrical socket could come out as well! It is not advisable to use electrical appliances from the US on this voltage system. If you are buying electrical appliances to take home, always check that they will work in your country before you buy.

FACILITIES FOR VISITORS WITH DISABILITIES

In all the newer shopping centres, hotels and complexes, there are facilities such as ramps, wider passageways, special lifts and toilets for visitors with disabilities. In the older areas it is a little more hit-and-miss, but on the whole you shouldn't have any problems. Most facilities are in the process of being updated according to EU specifications, and all pavements now have ramps for wheelchairs.

GETTING AROUND

Car hire Hiring a car in Gran Canaria is cheap, with many car rental firms at the airport, while others are based in and around the resorts. Shop around, as the prices can vary greatly, but it is an absolute must to have air-conditioning during the summer months. Most firms will give a total price, which includes insurance for personal accident, theft and breakdown – but always ask, never presume. All staff speak enough English for any enquiries. You can also book your car through an English company.
Autos Abroad Take a pre-paid voucher with you to the car rental firm at the airport or in the resort. ☎ 08700 667 788 (UK) ☎ 0208 496 499 (UK) Ⓦ www.autosabroad.com; or try **AutoEurope** ☎ 0800 032 1829 (UK) ☎ 00 353 16 59 05 50 (Spain) Ⓦ www.autoeurope.co.uk

When driving a hired car in Spain, all documents (insurance information, rental information and your driving licence) must be carried in the car. If stopped, the police require the originals, not photocopies, nor can you present your documents at a police station at a later date.

 Traffic within Las Palmas is busy and parking spaces impossible to find. Go by bus or on an organized trip.

Rules of the road Driving in Spain is not the same as in England. It is not just a matter of driving on the right. Watch the road signals carefully, give way to any traffic on roundabouts, don't be pushed into doing something because someone has his finger stuck on the hooter behind you, and be careful on some crossroads where, in order to turn left, you have first of all to turn right and then cross the road you were originally driving on.

The only fast roads on the island are the *autopista* (motorways), the GC1, GC2 and now, the GC3. The main route, the GC1, runs from Las Palmas down to the southern tip of the island at Puerto Rico. This one serves the airport. GC2 runs out of Las Palmas along the northern coast as far as Guia at present. The newly opened GC3 intersects at Jinamer on the GC1 and circumnavigates Las Palmas/Tamaraceite, heading north to join the GC2 to Guia. There is also a short section of GC3 motorway which goes off to Tafira Alta, from where you continue on the usual road to Santa Brigída/San Mateo. The speed limit on these roads is 120 km/h (75 mph), unless otherwise advised. On *carreteras* (dual carriageways) the limit is 80 km/h (50 mph), and in built-up areas it is 40 km/h (25 mph) or 30 km/h (19 mph). Motorists must carry their driving licence, passport, insurance and car-hire documents at all times. Failure to do so will result in an on-the-spot fine if stopped at one of the frequent road checks.

Road conditions The road surfaces are generally good, but many mountain roads are particularly narrow and winding. Nervous drivers might feel uncomfortable at first on some mountain roads, but safety barriers are well employed. Care and patience is all that is needed for safe driving.

Road markings These are generally clear but some of the traffic systems, especially those around motorway junctions, can be confusing when first encountered. Be aware that traffic priorities in these complex traffic systems do not always conform to European practice and you might suddenly find a stop sign on a main route.

Breaking down If your car does break down, in compliance with European Union laws, you must place red warning triangles 100 metres in front of and behind your vehicle. The police *will* fine you if you don't. Therefore it is always wise to check that you have them in your car. Then, all you need to do is to phone the 24-hour service number written on your insurance document or on the card which the car hire firm gives you, asking the representative if there are English-speaking people on the switchboard.

Buses There is an extremely good bus service, called Global, which runs buses all over the island. It has a 24-hour service going to and from Playa del Inglés to Las Palmas. Up to 23.00 hours, there are several buses per hour and they pass through Playa itself. After 23.00 hours, there is one bus per hour throughout the night until 06.00 hours, but this bus goes along the by-pass outside of Playa. The last bus from Mogán through Puerto Rico and on to Las Palmas leaves at 19.30 hours, the first bus in the morning leaves at 08.10 hours. From Las Palmas to Mogán, the first bus in the morning leaves at 05.40 hours and the last one leaves at 19.40 hours. If you want any other information about other bus routes and times, there are timetables on most bus stops, or you can go to the Global office in the Jumbo centre. Season tickets are available at the Jumbo centre if you think that you are going to make quite a few journeys on the same route. It is well worth looking into, because the saving is about 30 per cent.

If you intend travelling the same route fairly often, or if there are two or more of you, it pays to get a 'bono', which is a season ticket. You can buy them at the Jumbo centre in the shops with a Global sign, or at the bus station in Las Palmas. The Canarian word for bus is *guagua*, pronounced 'wah-wah'.

Taxis These are very reasonable and if there are more than two in your party, it could run out cheaper than going by bus. The best thing to do is to ask a taxi driver how much the fare would be to where you are going and then compare it with the bus fares.

EMERGENCY NUMBERS

For an ambulance or help in an emergency call:

Red Cross emergency service ☏ 222 222

Paramedics' freephone ☏ 061 or 112

Police ☏ 091

HEALTH MATTERS

Emergency dental and medical care Private clinics around the resorts are very well equipped for any medical or dental emergency, but if they cannot provide the necessary treatment, arrangements will be made to transfer you to a larger clinic or one of the hospitals. If you do not have private insurance but have a European Health Insurance Card, you must go directly to one of the National Health clinics or hospitals, remembering to take your passport with you. The standard of treatment and care is very high.

Private clinics Several private clinics with English-speaking staff offer 24-hour emergency medical assistance, including an ambulance service. For these clinics, take your flight tickets and travel insurance policy.

Medical Salud Las Palmeras ⓐ Avenida de Tenerife, Playa del Inglés ⓣ 928 76 29 92/93. They have a second location at: ⓐ Fase 2, Centro Civico Comercial Puerto Rico ⓣ 928 56 12 87

Clinica Roca A private hospital. ⓐ Buganvilla 1, San Agustín ⓣ 928 76 92 08/90 04

Health hazards Even with a breeze blowing, the sun is very strong and you should not stay out in it too long, especially between noon and 16.00 hours. Appropriate sun creams/blocks and sun apparel should be worn at all times.

Medicines If you have to take regular medication, always ensure that you bring enough to last for the duration of your stay. If you lose your medication and you have brought the leaflet or a repeat prescription, then a doctor/chemist will provide you with the same or equivalent drug.

Condoms Can be bought from any chemist, supermarket, other retail outlets and most mens' toilets.

Water While the local tap water in Gran Canaria will not kill you, it is not really advisable to drink it. The exception is in the town of Firgas (see page 24), which is famous for its spring water that is bottled and sold all over the island. You can buy it and other brands of bottled water from any of the supermarkets. For any other parts of the island, bottled water is recommended for making tea and coffee, and for cleaning your teeth.

THE LANGUAGE

The Canarians respond warmly to visitors who attempt to speak a little of their language. Here are a few words and phrases to get you going:

ENGLISH	SPANISH (pronunciation)
General vocabulary	
yes	*sí* (see)
no	*no* (no)
please	*por favor* (por faBOR)
thank you (very much)	*(muchas) gracias* ((MOOchas) GRAseeyas)
you're welcome	*de nada* (deNAda)
hello	*hola* (Ola)
goodbye	*adiós* (adeeYOS)
good morning/day	*buenos días* (BWEnos DEEyas)
good afternoon/evening	*buenas tardes* (BWEnas TARdes)
good evening (after dark)	*buenas noches* (BWEnas NOches)
excuse me (to get attention or to get past)	*¡disculpe!* (desKOOLpay)
excuse me (to apologize or to ask pardon)	*¡perdón!* (perDON)
sorry	*lo siento* (lo seeYENtoe)
Help!	*¡socorro!* (SOHcohroe)
	¡ayuda! (aiYUda)
today	*hoy* (oy)
tomorrow	*mañana* (manYAna)
yesterday	*ayer* (ayYER)
Useful words & phrases	
open	*abierto* (abeeYERtoe)
closed	*cerrado* (serRAdoe)
push	*empujar* (empooHA)
pull	*tirar* (teeRAR)
How much is it?	*¿Cuánto es?* (KWANtoe es)
expensive	*caro/a* (KARo/a)

ENGLISH
Useful words & phrases

| **SPANISH** (pronunciation) |

bank — *el banco* (el BANko)

bureau de change — *la oficina de cambio* (la ofeeSEEna de KAMbeeyo)

post office — *correos* (koRAYos)

duty (all-night) chemist — *la farmacia de guardia* (la farMAHseeya de garDEEya)

bank card — *la tarjeta de banco* (la tarHEHta deBANko)

credit card — *la tarjeta de crédito* (la tarHEHta de CREdeetoe)

traveller's cheques — *los cheques de viaje* (los CHEkes de beeAhay)

table — *la mesa* (la MEHsa)

menu — *el menú/la carta* (el menOO/la KARta)

waiter — *el/la camarero/a* (el/la kahmahRERo/a)

water — *agua* (Agwa)

fizzy/still water — *agua con/sin gas* (Agwa con/sin gas)

I don't understand. — *No entiendo* (No enteeYENdoe)

The bill, please. — *La cuenta, por favor* (la KWENta, porfaBOR)

Do you speak English? — *¿Habla usted inglés?* (Ablah OOsted eenGLES)

My name is... — *Me llamo ...* (meh YAmoh ...)

Where are the toilets? — *¿Dónde están los servicios?* (DONdeh esTAN los serVEEseeos)

Can you help me? — *¿Puede ayudarme?* (PWEday ayooDARmeh)

MEDIA

Newspapers Daily and Sunday papers can be bought in Gran Canaria from most large supermarkets and some kiosks.

Radio For UK news on the hour, sports and lottery results, as well as 24 hours of music, tune to QFM on FM98.

Television In any of the hotels or complexes that have televisions installed, you can usually get one or two English channels, normally Sky News and a Sky film channel. Football fans can watch league matches and all major tournament finals in most of the English bars.

OPENING HOURS

Banks Banks are open Monday to Friday from 08.30 to 14.00 hours, some on Saturday from 08.30 to 13.00 hours.

Churches If they are large, churches are open during the day until about 20.00 hours, but the smaller ones may only open during service hours and/or on Sundays.

Museums Museums are generally open daily from 09.00 to 19.30 hours, Monday to Saturday, but it is advisable to telephone and check.

Pharmacies Pharmacies have the same opening times as shops but do not open on Sunday. However, there is always a duty pharmacy open 24 hours a day somewhere in the area. In a resort the size of Playa, there are probably two or three that are open 24 hours. They rotate the duty days.

Restaurants Restaurants usually open daily and on public holidays as well.

Shops Most shops in the resorts open from 09.00 to 13.00 hours and 16.00 to 20.00 hours, Monday to Saturday, and some supermarkets open on a Sunday from 09.00 to 13.00 hours.

PERSONAL COMFORT & SECURITY

Crime Like in any other tourist resort, valuables left lying unattended or in cars are liable to be stolen. Men should not put their wallets in their back trouser pocket because there are pickpockets around. Women should avoid carrying a handbag with a strap over the shoulder because it could easily be snatched by someone running past or driving past on a motorbike. There is little incidence of violent crime on Gran Canaria.

TIMESHARE TOUTS
Touts can be a persistent nuisance in tourist areas. They are intent on persuading holidaymakers to visit and buy timeshare property. The best advice is to reject their advances, politely but firmly.

Laundry & dry-cleaning Most hotels/complexes have their own laundry facilities and if you speak to someone on reception, they will only be too happy to take your laundry and return it a day or two later, washed and ironed. Be warned though, your clothes will be mixed in with everything else and it isn't unusual to find that the colours have faded or changed, so don't give them your favourite clothing! There are some places where you can do your own washing and some hotel rooms even have their own washing machines. Dry-cleaners are called 'Tintorias'. They are good and very reasonable in price. Some hotels will even drop off your dry-cleaning and deliver it back to you.

Lost property Depending on where you lose it, you should first ask if it has been handed in. If it is something valuable or important, then you have to go to the police station (on the bypass, opposite the Hotel Buenaventura). Before going there however, contact the tour representative to ask them if they can provide you with an interpreter if you can't speak Spanish, or take someone who does, because the police will not deal with you if you do not speak the language. Remember, if your credit cards are stolen, you must contact their main office immediately to inform them and they will cancel them so that you lose as little money as possible.

Making a complaint If you have any complaints about the hotel/ complex, then it is always advisable to try and rectify it first with the staff and management. However, if nothing is done to alleviate the problem, then you should see your tour representative.

Police The local police (in blue uniforms) do not make their appearance too overpowering, but they do walk along the prom and drive around in efforts to prevent crime from happening. On the roads, you will see the traffic police, the Guardia Civil. They wear green uniforms and ride motorbikes or drive cars, and they take their job very seriously. The National Police wear navy trousers and jackets with white shirts. They deal with serious crime, murder, drug offences, etc.

Public toilets There are any number of public toilets in the resorts, in cafés, restaurants, shops and the airport. They are very clean and some have an attendent who will expect a small gratuity.

POST OFFICES

The post offices open Monday to Friday from 08.30 to 14.00 hours and on Saturdays from 08.30 to 13.00 hours. If you want to do anything other than post a letter or card, do it during the weekdays because all other transactions seem to shut down on a Saturday. The airport post office is not open on Saturdays.

RELIGION

There are religious buildings of all the major faiths on the island. In Playa there is the Ecumenical church in the main square, which holds services for Protestants and Roman Catholics. There is a Jehovah's Witness temple in San Fernando, Vecindario and Las Palmas. The Baptist and Non-Conformist churches are in Las Palmas, as is the mosque.

TELEPHONES

The island has an abundance of public telephones. Some take cards and some coins. You can also place a call from your hotel room, but beware of the cost involved. The cheapest time to call home is after 20.00 hours and all day Saturday and Sunday and public holidays. For the UK, dial 00 44 then the number, not forgetting to drop the 0 from the area code.

TIME DIFFERENCES

Because Gran Canaria is on the same line of longitude, the time is always the same as that of the UK. The clocks change in spring and autumn on the same day at the same time.

TIPPING

It isn't obligatory to tip and if you do, it should be because the meal and the service warrant it. The usual amount to leave is five to ten per cent of the total bill.

TOURIST INFORMATION

There are three main tourist offices on the island. They all have the same opening hours and website. 🕐 Mon–Fri 09.00–14.00, 15.00–20.00, Sat 09.00–13.00 (summer); Mon–Fri 09.00–22.00, Sat 09.00–13.00 (winter) 🌐 www.grancanaria.com

Playa del Inglés This tourist office is excellent, providing free maps and lots of local information, including printed bus timetables. 🅐 Avenida de España (adjacent to the Jumbo centre) 🕿 928 77 15 50 🖷 928 76 48 40

Las Palmas 🅐 Parque Santa Catalina 🕿 928 26 46 23 🖷 928 22 98 20

Puerto Rico 🅐 Centro Comercial 🕿 928 56 00 29

WEIGHTS & MEASURES

The official units of weights and measures are the kilo and the gram. All produce is sold like this.

Bars and restaurants here do not sell spirits, beers or wine according to official guidelines, so be careful, as you may find that a measure of whisky, for example, is much larger than the one you would receive back at home. Normally, the bartenders just pour until the glass is nearly full and then add a splash of the mixer of your choice!

Imperial to metric
1 inch = 2.54 centimetres
1 foot = 30 centimetres
1 mile = 1.6 kilometres
1 ounce = 28 grams
1 pound = 454 grams
1 pint = 0.6 litres
1 gallon = 4.6 litres

Metric to imperial
1 centimetre = 0.4 inches
1 metre = 3 feet, 3 inches
1 kilometre = 0.6 miles
1 gram = 0.04 ounces
1 kilogram = 2.2 pounds
1 litre = 1.8 pints

ACKNOWLEDGEMENTS

We would like to thank all the photographers, picture libraries and organisations for the loan of the photographs reproduced in this book, to whom copyright in the photograph belongs:
Brian and Eileen Anderson (pages 22, 55, 56, 58, 71, 72, 75, 80, 93, 94, 95);
Patricia Athie (page 16);
Pictures Colour Library Ltd (pages 15, 16, 46, 60, 62, 69, 76, 85, 86, 92, 96);
Copyright Thomas Cook (pages 1, 5, 13, 28, 32, 39, 43, 51, 65, 67, 83, 88, 98).

We would also like to thank the following for their contribution to this series:
John Woodcock (map and symbols artwork);
Becky Alexander, Patricia Baker, Sophie Bevan, Judith Chamberlain-Webber, Nicky Gyopari, Stephanie Horner, Krystyna Mayer, Robin Pridy (editorial support);
Christine Engert, Suzie Johanson, Richard Lloyd, Richard Peters, Alistair Plumb, Jane Prior, Barbara Theisen, Ginny Zeal, Barbara Zuñiga (Design support).

Send your thoughts to
books@thomascook.com

- **Found a beach bar, peaceful stretch of sand or must-see sight that we don't feature?**

- **Like to tip us off about any information that needs a little updating?**

- **Want to tell us what you love about this handy, little guidebook and more importantly how we can make it even handier?**

Then here's your chance to tell all! Send us ideas, discoveries and recommendations today and then look out for your valuable input in the next edition of this title. And, as an extra 'thank you' from Thomas Cook Publishing, you'll be automatically entered into our exciting monthly prize draw.

Email to the above address or write to:
HotSpots Project Editor, Thomas Cook Publishing, PO Box 227, Unit 15/16, Coningsby Road, Peterborough PE3 8SB, UK.